GRAND PRIX CARS

By

DENIS JENKINSON

New York

SPORTS CAR PRESS

CONTENTS

Page

Foreword 7

1. Birth of the Grand Prix 9

2. Those Muddled Pre-War Formulae 12

3. The First Post-War Champions 19

4. The Rise of Ferrari 35

5. Unsupercharged 1½ Litre vs. Supercharged 4½ Litre. . . 47

6. Formula 2 Comes to Stay 59

7. The Era of The Unhappy B.R.M. 68

8. 1954: How They Tackled The New Formula 80

9. The Short Happy Life of The Lancia 87

10. Mercedes Takes Over 92

11. The British Show Their Heads 102

12. Ferrari Has Troubles; Maserati Drops Out 105

13. How The Vanwall Came of Age 121

FOREWORD

In compiling this brief history of Grand Prix racing, along with descriptions of the more successful cars, I have limited myself to the period since World War II as the present day Grand Prix cars are mostly derived from the development and design of the early post war years. Although many ideas were taking shape in the period of the mid-thirties—such as the use of de Dion rear axle layouts, independent front suspension systems and hydraulic brakes—the main interest lay in engine design under a free ruling on capacity.

It was not until about 1950 that a renaissance began in chassis design for Grand Prix cars and from then on a great deal of knowledge was gained; enough in fact, to enable roadholding to become a very exact science rather than a hit-and-miss affair. This development in the chassis and the search for improved road holding and higher cornering power was accentuated by the beginning of the era of unsupercharged racing, when power outputs were severely curtailed and speed had to be found by other means.

Although the German cars of the 1934-39 period showed enormous technical advances, especially as regards engine design and supercharging knowledge, and provided some truly homeric racing, they look very crude and unimaginative beside the Grand Prix cars of today. In 1939 when European racing ceased for the war, the supercharged 1½-litre car, as exemplified by the quite small Alfa Romeo, was just beginning to show its possibilities on a fast but twisty circuit in comparison with the big Grand Prix cars of that time, as witness the Swiss Grand Prix of 1939, or the comparison of the 1938 and 1939 Tripoli Grand Prix events.

Had the war years not intervened, the trend towards smaller and more manageable Grand Prix cars would have followed, so that when this happened during the postwar period it was nothing more than natural evolution. For these reasons, the period of Grand Prix racing from 1946-58 can be looked at as a single phase in the development of the Grand Prix car, and for that reason I have dwelt mainly on that period.   *Denis Jenkinson,*
Hampshire, England.

1. BIRTH OF THE GRAND PRIX

Before we look too closely into the whys and wherefores of Grand Prix cars, and make a study of the various types and makes, let us first discuss the words Grand Prix. Of French origin, they mean literally, Great Prize, and the equivalent in Italian is *Gran Premio,* in German *Grosser Preis,* in Dutch *Grotj Prij,* and so on in almost any language. It is only in English (and American) that the equivalent two words of that language are not used; we have traditionally preferred the French words, Grand Prix.

This is probably due to the close connections socially and geographically between England and France, and America has followed England's lead. In continental circles the term Grand Prix is used for many things apart from motor car racing, and the name *Grand Prix d'honneur,* or Honorable Great Prize can be, and is, applied to such varied things as cake making, dress design, and wine making. So it is easy to see that the original use of the term Grand Prix in connection with automobile racing was applied to the best performance, and subsequently to the best race, and the name Grand Prix Car was given to any car competing for the Great Prize.

Although the first motor competition was held in 1894 and the first motor race in 1895, it was not until 1906 that the title of Grand Prix was given to an event. Between these dates many motor races took place and the principal events were undoubtedly those for the Gordon Bennett Cup, an award put up by a great sportsman of the early 1900's and competed for annually. In the early days of racing the classification of the competing cars was pretty much free-for-all, but from 1902—and specifically for the Gordon Bennett race—the competing cars had to comply with a formula decided upon by an International body of representatives from those countries interested in motor racing. This body was based in Paris, the capital city of the first country to hold a motor race.

By 1906 the Gordon Bennett race was losing favor and the principal race of the year was named the Grand Prix, this being the first time that the term was applied to motor racing, and the cars competing in this event had to comply with a rule which stipulated a maximum weight of 1000 kilogrammes, or 2200 lbs. From that date onwards the International Formula for racing cars and the name Grand Prix have been synonymous. But already a complication was beginning, for countries other than France were organizing motor races, and both Germany and Italy held an important race in 1907 which they considered to be of equal importance to the Grand Prix.

As if to confuse the issue even more, the German race, the *Kaiserpreis,* and the Italian race, the *Targa Florio,* were both run according to their own special regulations, so that any manufacturer who wanted to compete in all three events was forced to build three different cars. With France being the instigator and still the leader of motor racing, the 1907 Grand Prix Formula can be considered the important one, and it merely limited fuel consumption to 9.4 miles per gallon. The following year, 1908, the French decreed that their Grand Prix should be run according to a limit of piston area, this being a maximum of 117 sq. ins., leaving the number of cylinders, and bore and stroke choice entirely open.

The cost of building these special cars for the major race of the year was by now becoming rather exhorbitant, and after the 1908 Grand Prix the manufacturers got together and decided to abstain from any further Grand Prix racing. In consequence of this no Grand Prix was held in the following two years, and in 1911 a very mediocre and poorly supported Grand Prix was held.

In the meantime racing had continued for smaller cars, for while the Grand Prix proper was in being there were always other races for a class of car known as "voiture legere" or "voiturette"—which is to say, light cars. The cars built to the Grand Prix formulae were inevitably and by definition the biggest and best, though not always the fastest, even though they were intended to be, and the voiturette class was only considered as a subsidiary to the Great Prize category.

When the manufacturers forced the abandonment of the Grand Prix in 1909, the light cars continued to race and their regulations and limitations formulated racing and design for many years, even though the Grand Prix was revived in 1912. For this year the formula was thrown wide open with no restrictions, the French title being Formula Libre, and this was done in the hope of attracting the maximum number of entries. This it did, and whereas Fiat and Lorraine entered monster cars of 15 litres, whose design dated back to the last Grand Prix of 1908, Peugeot entered comparatively small cars of only 7.6 litres engine capacity—their design stemming directly from the previous two years of voiturette racing.

In this free-for-all of 1913 the little Peugeots were victorious, and this made designers realize that mere engine capacity was not necessarily all it took to win races. For 1913 the French went back to fuel consumption formula, this time of 14 m.p.g., their apparent desire all the time being to limit the performance of the Grand Prix racing cars, as every year they felt that cars were becoming too fast. In fact, the cry from the French Automobile Club of "too fast" has come from Paris since the very beginning of motor racing, and persists even today.

In 1914 the Grand Prix was run to a more realistic formula which put a definite limit on engine size, this being $4\frac{1}{2}$ litres, a good compromise figure in view of the results of the 1912 and 1913 Grand Prix races, for the former was won by a Peugeot with an engine size of 7.6 litres and the latter by another Peugeot of 5.6 litres. Then, of course, just as Grand Prix racing was beginning to take some definite form, war broke out and all racing ceased.

2. THOSE MUDDLED PRE-WAR FORMULAE

While the title of Grand Prix was being given to the major French race of the year, this does not mean that it was the only important race. The sport of motor racing was spreading throughout the world, the Vanderbilt Cup races starting in 1904 on Long Island, and in the early days most of the races were between major French towns, such as Paris-Rouen, Paris-Dieppe, Nice-Marseilles, Bordeaux-Biarritz, etc., while in Belgium the Ardennes races were beginning to set the fashion for circuit racing, or racing round a predetermined course rather than from one town to another. In 1908 America held a race to the French formula of that year, limiting piston area, and this was held at Savannah, while in 1911 the famous Indianapolis Speedway began its long list of 500-mile races.

As can be seen, the original idea of the Grand Prix race was soon becoming confused, for quite rightly the French had chosen this title for their own major race of the year. And equally rightly, the other countries also felt justified in giving a similar title to their major race. 1908 can be considered the first year of the true Grand Prix race, which is to say, a race run under the Formula drawn up for the French Grand Prix of that year.

As already mentioned, the American Grand Prix was run at Savannah under the 117 sq. in. piston area limit, and in Siciliy the Coppa Florio was run to this regulation. Therefore, for our purposes we can say that a Grand Prix is a race run according to the Formula laid down by the International body in Paris, and a Grand Prix car is one that complies to this Formula. This may seem rather elementary and obvious, but after the 1914-18 war the term Grand Prix began to be used for races that did not comply with the exist-

12

ing Formula, and in 1923 when the Le Mans 24-hour race was begun, the major award was for the *Grand Prix d'Endurance,* which was reasonable and self-explanatory, but did nothing to clarify the position of the term Grand Prix as applied to motor racing.

Although racing began again in 1919 at Indianapolis, it was not until 1921 that the first post-war Grand Prix was held in Europe. Taking a lead from the 1920 Indianapolis 500-mile race, the European Grand Prix Formula was for cars of 3 litres capacity, with the addition of a minimum weight limit of 800 kilograms, (or 1763 lbs). France held her most important race to this Formula, as did Italy, and these two races were the true beginning of the revival of Grand Prix racing, and were considered along with Indianapolis of that year, which also ran to the Formula, to be the most important and the highest standard of motor racing.

Subsequently the term Grand Prix was to apply to races of lesser standing, including many that did not comply with the International Formula—and was even used for the first sports car race—but in the following descriptions of Grand Prix cars it is assumed that the term applies only to those events run under the current Formula decided by the representatives of the various national automobile clubs. There is no hard and fast rule or law to say what shall or shall not be called a Grand Prix race, and both in Europe and America, races for unlimited sports cars are still run under the title of Grand Prix, the basic idea being that they are the Great Prize as far as that particular country or circuit are concerned, whereas it all began on the erroneous assumption that all countries would hold their most important event to an agreed Formula.

From a purely academic point of view we shall consider Grand Prix cars only as those designed and built around the various Formulae, whose rules were changed every few years seemingly in the light of previous experience, but more often that not through the eternal unending French cry of "too fast." In order that readers can get a sound basic knowledge of the development of the Grand Prix racing car, it is worth spending a little more space on enumerating the various Formulae over the years 1920-1939, but space will not permit of detailed descriptions of the many cars built, which are now only of historic interest.

However, we shall look closely into the various cars built to the Formulae since the end of World War II up to the present day, for though Grand Prix racing has been exceedingly active over the past 11 years and the cars of 1947 are now bordering on the historic, they have influenced the design and conception of the Grand Prix car as we know it today.

Indianapolis Drops Out

For the years 1922-1925 the Formula for Grand Prix cars was a simple one, limiting the engine capacity to 2 litres, and for 1926 and 1927 this maximum limit was reduced to 1.5 litres. From 1928 to 1933 the world-wide economic depression caused European racing to slip into a dull period, and Grand Prix races were run to any Formula the organizers liked to think up, though officially in 1928 the Formula imposed weight limits of between 550 and 750 kilograms and race distances of 600 kilometres.

As this did not prove popular, 1929 saw a new set of regulations which called for a fuel consumption limit, a minimum body width of 39 inches, a minimum weight of 1800 lbs. and other rather fatuous body regulations. It was not surprising that this proved even less acceptable to manufacturers, and most of the races continued to be run outside the rules. In fact, Indianapolis, which had stuck with the European Formula up to 1927 and continued it for 1928 and 1929, now abandoned all hope of ever agreeing to the International Formula and, in 1930, threw the 500-mile race open to cars up to 6 litres capacity. Meanwhile the European organizers and constructors had overruled the governing body and races were being run to a Formula Libre, even though the 1929 Formula was supposed to have continued in force in 1930, with very slight alterations regarding the fuel to be used.

The apparent control of motor racing, in Europe anyway, was still supposedly in the hands of a body comprising delegates from each country interested in racing. This body was known as the

Association Internationale des Automobile Clubs Reconnu, later to be renamed the *Federation Internationale Automobile*, or F.I.A. Whereas in the early days the A.I.A.C.R. was very much in touch with the organizers and car constructors, it was very obvious that by 1930 this apparently democratic body had become something of a despot and had its head in the sand as far as prevailing conditions in the industry were concerned.

After the complete failure of the 1928-29 and 1930 Formulae, they continued to flounder about and for 1931 decreed a maximum engine capacity of 5 litres, superchargers were banned, and a scale of weights of 20.8 kilograms per 100 cc over and above an absolute minimum of 794 kilograms was imposed. There were also detail limitations on chassis and body dimensions, the idea being to encourage the building of a racing car that bore some resemblance to an everyday motorcar. This was a fine and noble thought on paper, but quite uninteresting to those people who were interested in motor racing. The result was a complete lack of response from car builders, who all saw in the racing car a mechanized device for travelling at faster and faster speeds, untrammelled by equipment or limits that were not calculated to increase the speed of the vehicle.

It is easy to see why Indianapolis lost all interest in the A.I.A.C.R. and began the development of pure racing machinery whose one object was to go faster than ever before. Realizing that their new Formula was yet another flop, the A.I.A.C.R. gave in and scrapped all the rules, throwing Grand Prix racing open to any size or type of car, with the proviso that the body was of two-seater width and that races should be of 10 hours duration. As this meant that all the Formula Libre cars could now qualify there was something of a truce called, and Grand Prix racing began to revive. And when in 1932 the A.I.A.C.R. at last took heed of the demands of those people directly interested in racing by reducing the length of races from 10 hours to 5 hours, and scrapped the two-seater body width rule, there was general agreement all around. However, the damage done in 1928 which sent Indianapolis away from the European trends was irrevocable and the 500-mile race and Grand Prix racing continued on their own separate ways. This was a great pity, for in the years 1921-1927 there had been very definite agreement between both sides of the Atlantic, and it was ruined only by the bungling of the decisions made in Paris.

For 1933 the basic Formula Libre rules still applied but, due to this free hand in design, manufacturers such as Bugatti, Alfa Romeo and Maserati were beginning to settle upon a compromise of design that was proving highly satisfactory to all concerned. After experimenting with engines as large as 5 litres, and twin-engined cars, in the search for more and more power at the expense of chassis and road holding research, they all came to the conclusion that an engine size of somewhere around 3 litres was commensurate with a reasonably proportioned and balanced single-seater racing car, and that attention to road holding provided a greater increase in lap speeds than sheer power. In consequence, the A.I.A.C.R. produced a set of rules for 1934 that were based on the findings of the racing manufacturers in 1932.

The Germans Outfox The A.I.A.C.R.

Already the Grand Prix cars were capable of speeds approaching 150 m.p.h., and though the Paris body took heed of the racing car developments of the past years, they were still worried that cars were "too fast." The new rules imposed a maximum weight limit of 750 kilograms (1650 lbs) and deemed that races should be run for at least 500 kilometres (310 miles). The thinking behind these rules was that the weight imposition would keep engine sizes down to about $2\frac{1}{2}$ to 3 litres and the distance would ensure a freak of say 6 litres in an absurdly light chassis would last only a few minutes and thus would not be built. These rules were drawn up in the light of the knowledge of design of racing cars and metallurgy existent at that time in France and Italy, the two major powers in European racing, but when the 1934 season got under way and new cars from Germany, built by Daimler-Benz and a new firm called Auto-Union, joined in, it was soon obvious that these firms had out-smarted the old gentlemen in Paris.

By extensive use of light alloys, and keeping the stress on every component down to an absolute minimum, both these German designs appeared with engines of 4 litres and more, and all hope of the new Formula limiting speeds was lost. This Formula lasted for the years 1934 to 1937, during which time engine sizes exceeded 6 litres and yet the cars still weighed less than the minimum of 1650 lbs—less fuel, oil and tires—and could last a full length Grand Prix race, while speeds had risen to nearly 190 m.p.h.

For 1938 a return was made to a limitation on engine capacity, as well as a retention of weight limits, only this time a minimum weight limit was imposed. With superchargers the engines could not exceed 3 litres, and without superchargers they could be as large as $4\frac{1}{2}$ litres, but for both capacities the cars had to weigh at least 850 kilograms (1870 lbs). In this way it was felt that the fantastic speeds achieved in 1937 would be reduced to reasonable proportions. For once an A.I.A.C.R. Formula achieved its objective and, not only that, it transferred designers attention to the important subject of chassis design and roadholding. By 1939 this new Formula was producing Grand Prix cars that could lap most circuits at higher average speeds than the 1937 cars, in spite of having only half the engine capacity, additional weight, and a loss of some 20 m.p.h. on maximum speed.

The reason for this was simply the ability of the cars to go round corners at higher speeds and to brake more efficiently, these two factors more than outweighing a loss in maximum speed and acceleration. Taken all round, the 1938-39 Grand Prix cars were much more controllable and in consequence the drivers could use the car's potential much more of the time with the subsequent rise in lap speeds, which after all is the main objective of a racing driver. With this very reasonable Grand Prix Formula, the Indianapolis organizers returned to a European way of thinking and adopted the engine capacity limits for the 500-mile race, but unfortunately the years between 1928 and 1938 had seen Indianapolis branch off on its own, with complete justification, so that it had become highly specialized in comparison with the European trend of design.

Though 1938 saw the two types of racing running under the same Formula, the prevailing conditions on the two sides of the Atlantic were such that the cars bore little or no resemblance. However, in 1939 a pure Grand Prix car won at Indianapolis, and again in 1940, by which time of course, World War II had put a stop to all European racing. The Maserati which won at Indianapolis, driven by Wilbur Shaw, was an out-and-out Grand Prix car and one of the major contenders in European racing in 1939, and undoubtedly this car influenced the design of Indianapolis cars from that year onwards.

History had repeated itself, for in 1914 Grand Prix racing was just getting settled down after some stormy years when war put a stop to all activity, and in 1939 the same thing happened. Whereas the revival of racing in 1919 saw a fresh start being made, the design and development of the automobile having progressed during the war years, the second revival in 1946 saw a continuation, as far as Europe was concerned, with what was left over from 1939.

3. THE FIRST POST-WAR CHAMPIONS

For the purposes of this survey we will look more closely at the cars that were the most successful or the most interesting in the years following World War II up to the present, at the same time noting the changes made in the International Formula for Grand Prix racing, and seeing how there has been continual development in the racing car through the years.

As we have seen, the 1938-39 Formula was successfully reducing the maximum speeds of the cars, but improvements in chassis design and roadholding were allowing increases in lap speeds, which was an obvious technical improvement, while the b.h.p. being produced per litre of engine capacity was also increasing. In 1939 the German firms of Mercedes-Benz and Auto-Union were all-conquering in Grand Prix racing, though Alfa Romeo, Maserati, Bugatti, Delahaye and Talbot had been making half-hearted attempts to prevent this German domination.

Naturally, 1946 saw Germany in no position to begin motor racing again, even though the 1939 Mercedes-Benz cars were still in existence, as was most of the Daimler-Benz racing organization, whereas Auto-Union was disbanded and gone for ever. In Italy, in 1939 and in 1940 the Alfa Romeo firm had begun racing small 1½-litre Alfa Romeos in "voiturette" racing, as they could make no impression in Grand Prix events with their 3-litre cars, so it was not surprising to see these Type 158 Alfa Romeos produced again in 1946. Together with 1½-litre Maseratis that had survived the war years, these two makes of car revived racing in Italy.

In France there still existed a few Talbot and Delahaye cars of 4½-litres unsupercharged capacity and these, together with a varied collection of older cars, formed the beginnings of the resumption of motor racing. For 1946 there were only a very few events, and the entries were made up from any vehicle that could be made to run and for which tires existed. But by 1947, the situation in Europe looked more promising. The A.I.A.C.R. had been reformed and renamed the *Federation Internationale Automobile*, or F.I.A. for short, and they decided on a simple Formula for Grand Prix racing, to take effect from the beginning of 1947 and to last for three years. This stipulated a maximum engine size of 1½ litres if a supercharger was used or 4½ litres if unsupercharged. This Formula came about mainly through a sensible assessment of the cars available for racing in 1946 and to some degree through the knowledge gained in 1938-39. In that period of 3 litres supercharged and 4½ litres unsupercharged, all the powerful firms such as Daimler-Benz, Auto-Union, Maserati and Alfa Romeo had put all their technical knowledge into the problem of the 3-litre supercharged engine, achieving as much as 485 b.h.p. from such a capacity, while the 4½-litres unsupercharged limit was only tackled by small firms such as Talbot and Delahaye. The result was that the best unsupercharged engine of those days gave only 250 b.h.p., and the only hope of beating the supercharged cars lay in better fuel consumption, allowing races to be completed non-stop while their more powerful rivals had to refuel half-way through and lose precious seconds at the pits. On a few rare occasions this state of affairs allowed the unsupercharged 4½-litre cars to win, but generally speaking they were so outclassed on speed that it was very obvious that there was no real equality between the two engine limits.

In 1939 when Alfa Romeo appeared with their very advanced 8-cylinder supercharged 1½-litre car it proved as fast as the big 4½-litres and on certain circuits not a great deal slower than the 3-litre cars. It is easy to see why the 1947 Formula was decided upon, for apart from availability of cars, it followed the trend that was being indicated in 1939, where a 1½-litre supercharged engine was producing nearly as much power as the existing unsupercharged 4½-litre engines. Bearing in mind that no one had made a very serious attempt at designing a 4½-litre engine, most of

20

them being developed from sports car engines, it seemed likely that the new Formula would see more equality between the two types of car.

The All-Conquering 158 Alfa Romeo

1947 saw the Alfa Romeo team in complete command of Grand Prix racing, their only serious rivals being Maserati and Talbot, though there were numerous other competitiors with E.R.A., Alta, and Delahaye cars. The Italian Alfa Romeo team was undoubtedly the best organized and able to put the most into racing, and its 8-cylinder cars underwent some very good development. The engine had a bore and stroke of 58x70 mm, giving a capacity of 1479 cc, and was supercharged by a Roots instrument mounted alongside the engine and driven by an open shaft from the timing gears at the front of the block. Two overhead gear-driven camshafts were used, and the engine ran to 8000 r.p.m., developing nearly 200 b.h.p.

This engine was mounted in a simple chassis frame consisting of two large diameter tubular side members with tubular cross members. A four-speed gearbox built-in unit with the differential assembly formed the transmission and was mounted on the rear end of the chassis, a thin propellor shaft connecting the engine to the gearbox. Suspension to all four wheels was independent, that at the front being by trailing arms, like a Volkswagen, but using a transverse leaf spring, and at the rear swing axles were used, again with a transverse leaf spring. Very large hydraulic brakes were fitted to all wheels, and a compact single-seater body was used with a large fuel tank in the tail. It is interesting that this car was of a very similar layout to the large 3-litre car built by Alfa Romeo in 1938, which had a V16 cylinder engine, the small car engine being in effect one bank of cylinders from the vee engine.

In 1947 and the following years this Alfa Romeo, known as the Type 158, was to become the standard at which everyone aimed when building 1½-litre supercharged Grand Prix cars. It's closest rival was the 4CL Maserati, a fairly straightforward and simple car, built with far less reources by the Maserati brothers in their Bologna workshops. This car had a 4-cylinder engine with two overhead camshafts, and was supercharged by a Roots blower mounted in front of the block. It was mounted in a chassis comprising two box-sectioned side members, braced by an elektron oil tank that bolted into the chassis to form a rigid center cross member. Front suspension was by double wishbones and longitudinal torsion bars, while at the rear a rigid one-piece axle was mounted on $\frac{1}{4}$-elliptic leaf springs, which was rather a primitive layout. A four-speed gearbox was mounted directly on the rear of the engine, with an open propellor shaft to the rear axle, and, like Alfa Romeo, this Maserati was developed in 1938-39 from the 3-litre Maserati of the type which had won at Indianapolis two years running.

Both these $1\frac{1}{2}$-litre cars, which formed the backbone of 1947 racing, had been evolved just before the war from experience gained in full Grand Prix racing of that time, and had come about because the Italians realized that they could not compete against the powerful German teams. Both Alfa Romeo and Maserati built these $1\frac{1}{2}$-litre cars, and all Italian races in 1939 were run under a special Italian Formula with a limit of $1\frac{1}{2}$ litres, decided on specifically to keep the German cars out.

During 1947 plans were made in England and France to build new Grand Prix cars, to supplement the old pre-war E.R.A.'s and Talbots that were being raced, while in Italy the new firm of Ferrari was beginning to make itself noticed. Alfa Romeo continued to win all the major Grand Prix events, while the smaller races were inevitably won by Maserati, so that between the two of them they made sure that Italy was supreme in Grand Prix racing in 1947 and again in 1948. The 158 Alfa Romeo had not undergone any major changes, but the engine power was increased enormously by the fitting of two-stage supercharging, the two blowers being in tandem on the left side of the engine, with the rearmost one being the first stage and drawing from a special triple-choke Weber carburetor.

Wherever the Alfa Romeo team appeared in 1947 and 1948 they were practically assured of first place, and more often than

Start of French Grand Prix 1949 at Rheims with 4 CLT/48 Maserati and 1½-litre Ferrari leading

23

Alberto Ascari in a 1948 Maserati 4 CLT/48 supercharged 1500cc 4 cylinder Grand Prix car

Maserati 4 CLT/48 engine. Two overhead camshafts, four valves per cylinder, eight exhaust pipes, two shuperchargers

not they finished 1st, 2nd and 3rd, while on some special occasions they entered four cars and posted a 1-2-3-4 finishing order. Maserati also developed their supercharging system on the 4CL engine, fitting two Roots supercharges one above the other in front of the engine in a two-stage layout. In addition they redesigned the chassis frame, using tubular side members, though front and rear suspension remained unaltered, and though they were the chief rivals to the Alfa Romeo team, they never succeeded in conquering them.

With Europe returning to a more stable condition, the year 1948 saw Grand Prix racing increasing in popularity. Many new cars appeared and many more new designs were begun, but in spite of all the activity, the Alfo Romeo team were not unduly worried, though they did bring out an improved version known as the Type 158A, this being more highly developed as regards engine and brakes and giving over 300 b.h.p. from the highly supercharged $1\frac{1}{2}$ litres capacity. The chassis and suspension were still considered to be adequate and no changes were made.

Maserati, on the other hand, underwent a major change in the chassis in 1948, just after the Maserati brothers sold the firm to the Orsi family who moved the activities to Modena. The new car was known as the 4 CLT/48 and had an entirely new tubular chassis layout and front suspension by means of double wishbones and coil springs, the spring being mounted inboard of the wishbone pivots and an extension from the top wishbone compressing the spring as the wheel rose. The engine, gearbox and rear axle remained unaltered from the 1947 cars, as did the rear suspension, though the $\frac{1}{4}$-elliptic springs were splayed out more on the new car.

The whole car was a great deal lower than its predecessors and had a distinctive flat and bulbous radiator cowling and a rather high tail, which was the fuel tank. The engine still retained the square bore and stroke measurements, of 78x78 mm, and the large lower supercharger still fed into the smaller second stage blower mounted above it, both still being in front of the engine. The four-speed gearbox drove by open propellor shaft to the one-piece rear axle, but this now had a pair of step-up gears on the nose of

1948 Alfa Romeo Type 158 being driven by Farina

the pinion housing in order that the transmission line could be lowered, consequently lowering the driver's seat and overall height of the car. These 1948 Maseratis were quite successful cars, and though they were never able to beat the Alfa Romeo cars for 1st place they often broke up the Alfa Romeo monopoly, frequently finishing 2nd or 3rd.

The Unsuccessful Alta

From England, in 1948, there appeared a newcomer to the Grand Prix field in the shape of a lone Alta, this being built by a small firm near London. While it was of advanced design in many features, it suffered from a lack of development brought about by limited finances. This car had a four-cylinder engine of the same dimensions as the Maserati, but it had only two valves per cylinder against the Italian car's four valves, and the Alta camshafts, mounted in the cylinder head were driven by a single roller chain. Only one-stage supercharging was used to begin with, this being of the popular Roots type, using two revolving paddles, and whereas the Italian supercharged cars used Weber carburetors, the English car used S.U. carburetors. A four-speed synchromesh gearbox was bolted to the rear of the engine and this drove to a rear axle unit bolted to the rear of the tubular chassis frame. All four wheels were independently sprung by using double wishbones, the bottom one having a bell-crank lever which compressed a solid block of rubber when the wheel rose. These rubber blocks, there being one for each wheel, were housed in the tubular cross members, while the upper wishbones had hydraulic shock absorbers attached to their pivot spindles.

This Alta competed in a number of the Grand Prix races during 1948, but never succeeded in overcoming small troubles and was unable to develop enough power with its single supercharger to challenge the Italian cars. By now it was clear that the supercharged 1½-litre Grand Prix car was the most popular line of design, and that engine power was all important, and this was a direct product of available supercharger pressure. Most people were using the Roots type supercharger and obtained high pressures either by increasing the rotational speeds, using extremely large superchargers, or by fitting a two-stage system.

However, another car that was nearing completion in England was the B.R.M. The initials stood for British Racing Motors, a firm supported by numerous non-racing concerns. This car was breaking new ground in a number of ways, the most significant being the use of 16 cylinders in vee formation, for their 1½-litres capacity, and the use of centrifugal superchargers in two stages, in order to obtain very high pressures without the power loss that the Roots type involved when it was giving similar pressures. Extremely high power outputs were being obtained by the B.R.M. while on test, but it was quite some time before the car was ready

The 1500cc supercharged Alta Grand Prix car of 1948

to race, there being much experimental work to do with regard to brakes and suspension, both of which were unorthodox, while the whole car was very complicated and even the simplest job of maintenance took far longer than was justifiable.

Another new and complicated car appeared in France about this time, designed by M. Lory and built by the *Centre d'Etudes Technique de l'Automobile,* and most of the manufacture of the parts was done in the French Government Arsenal. The car was known as the C.T.A.-Arsenal, and was a 1½-litre V-8 of 60x65.6 mm bore and stroke, had two overhead camshafts to each bank of cylinders, two spark plugs per cylinder and two-stage supercharging by Roots-type blowers.

The engine was fairly conventional in design and somewhat agricultural in construction, much of it being of cast-iron, and altogether the C.T.A.-Arsenal was not a success—having been built with limited financial backing and being operated by a group of people with very little racing experience. The car made but one appearance in 1948, and that was a complete failure because it broke a drive-shaft on the starting line. By the end of the season a second car was completed but by this time chaos reigned in the organization, money was running out, and the whole project was doomed before it got going.

A Champ Is Born

While these new supercharged 1½-litre cars were being designed and built in England and France, yet another new make was under way in Italy. Where the B.R.M., Alta and C.T.A.-Arsenal were to prove comparative failures, the new Italian firm was to achieve untold success. The firm in question was controlled and organized by Enzo Ferrari, a name connected with motor racing since the early 1920's, and active in the pre-war years with a team of Alfa Romeo cars. Since 1946 Ferrari had been building his own sports cars, as Alfa Romeo was running its own racing team and the 158

Two 1949 Ferrari Grand Prix cars driven by Ascari and Villoresi. 12 cylinder 1500cc supercharged engines

Alfa Romeos were not for sale. By the end of the 1948 season Ferrari had built his first Grand Prix car, a supercharged 1½-litre with a V-12 cylinder engine based on his successful 2-litre, 12-cylinder sports car engines.

This new car was very compact and short, had independent suspension to all four wheels, used a single supercharger for its engine and only one camshaft to each bank of cylinders, the inclined valves being operated by rockers. The bore and stroke were 55x52.5 mm being of the "over-square" type, pioneered by Daimler-Benz in 1939 on their 1500cc racing car, and to become an essential design feature in racing engines. The new Ferrari was quite powerful, developing 230 b.h.p. Being light it had a good performance, but its roadholding and handling left a lot to be desired, as did its reliability.

However, in its initial races it proved to be more than a match for the 4CLT/48 Maserati, but not quite the equal of the 158 Alfa Romeo, so that racing became very interesting at the end of 1948 with these three leading Italian makes with their supercharged 1½-litre cars vying for the first three places. With the supercharged Alta, B.R.M. and C.T.A.-Arsenal in experimental stages, racing seemed to be on a very firm footing, especially as regards the highly supercharged small engine.

At the same time, another project in this category was nearing completion in Italy—the rear-engined Cisitalia—a revolutionary design from the drawing board of Dr. Porsche which had a horizontally opposed 12-cylinder engine and five-speed gearbox mounted behind the driver. Independent suspension to all four wheels was used, and provision was made for the drive from the engine to go to all four wheels, for acceleration purposes, or to the rear wheels only, for cornering purposes, the choice being made by the driver with a hand lever on the steering column. This car was in the category of the B.R.M. and C.T.A.-Arsenal in being too complicated and too costly for the people behind the project, the Cisitalia firm being a small private concern in Turin that built sports cars.

All this while the successful Alfa Romeo team was continuing to

The Lago-Talbot 4500cc 6 cylinder unsupercharged Grand Prix of 1948-51

win all the big races and the supercharged 1½-litre side of the Formula had the greatest following. There was only one protagonist for the 4½-litre unsupercharged school of thought and that was Anthony Lago, who was building the rather large and cumbersome 6-cylinder Lago-Talbot, which was too heavy and underpowered to be of any real opposition to the small supercharged cars.

The Lago-Talbot engine was developed from sports car knowledge, having overhead valves operated by short pushrods and rockers, the camshafts being set high up in the cylinder block. The chassis design was rather primitive, front suspension being independent, but the rear axle was a one-piece affair mounted on large half-elliptic leaf springs. The only points in favor of the Lago-Talbot were its reliability and its good fuel consumption, which meant that it could run a full race without refueling where the highly supercharged cars had to stop at least once. Like Maserati, the Lago-Talbot was for sale and quite a number of these cars were raced by private-owners, to whom this reliability factor was very important.

With the opening of the 1949 season, prospects for Grand Prix racing looked as bright as ever they had been. Alfa Romeo, Maserati and Ferrari all had first class teams, numerous Lago-Talbots were in the hands of non-factory drivers, some of the old pre-war English E.R.A. cars were still in the running and new projects were about to blossom forth. From a design point of view, especially as regards engines, it was one of the most varied periods in Grand Prix racing, there being supercharged cars with 4 cylinders, 8 cylinders, V-8 cylinders, V-12, flat-12 and V-16 cylinder arrangements while every possible trend of design was being followed in respect to such details as superchargers, carburetors, plugs, valves and valve-gear and camshafts.

Alfa Romeo Retires

With the season almost begun, Alfa Romeo suddenly announced that they would not be racing during 1949 and they withdrew the entire 158 team, put them under dust-sheets and refused to lend the cars or sell them. Their reason for retirement was the desire to reorganize the factory for the future production of a new series of road cars, which we now know to have been the Giulietta and the various 2-litre 4-cylinder models. In addition to this production work at the Milan factory, it had been obvious during 1948 that the Alfa Romeos were practically assured of winning any races they entered, and the directors of the firm did not feel justified in going on spending enormous sums of money to race without there being any serious opposition. Although Ferrari and Maserati occasionally challenged the Alfa Romeo team, neither of them had actually beaten the Milan team so there was some justification in Alfa Romeos withdrawal.

This left the Grand Prix field to Maserati and Ferrari, and it was not long before it became obvious that Maserati was going to come out on top. The 4 CLT/48 Maserati was only a modification of an old design and was fast becoming obsolete, while the Grand Prix Ferrari was just getting over its prototype troubles and starting on a successful period of development. So, it was not surprising that as the season progressed Ferrari became more and more the master of Grand Prix racing. The interesting projects from England and France never did get under way, while the Cisitilia firm went broke before their car ever reached the starting line, so that the only opposition to the two Italian firms came from the Talbots—whose only hope lay in their economy and ability to do a "tortoise and hare" act, which occasionally came off.

From what seemed to be an exciting beginning, the year 1949 ended with Ferrari leading the field in race winning and in design, all the hoped-for opposition having fallen by the wayside due to complexity of design being too much for the organization behind the team, a lack of money, or a too-slow rate of development. By the end of the season Ferrari had designed a new car, longer and heavier than the original Grand Prix car and having two overhead camshafts to each of the banks of cylinders and two-stage super-charging. Whereas Maserati was prepared to sell the 4CLT/48 model to almost any driver, Ferrari was not so keen, though he could be persuaded to sell his earlier cars to those whom he considered the "right people."

It is interesting to recall that in 1949 one of his early short-chassis models was sold to a Mr. G. A. Vandervell who raced it in England under the name of "Thinwall Special" and it is doubtful whether anyone at that time could forsee the possible outcome of this activity. At this time Mr. Vandervell was still connected with the B.R.M. project, though he was rapidly becoming dissatisfied with the way the B.R.M. organization was conducting itself, and this purchase of the Ferrari, to be driven by various well-known drivers, eventually led to his leaving B.R.M., setting up his own racing team, and finally building his own magnificent car.

4. THE RISE OF FERRARI

In 1950 Alfa Romeo announced that they would return to racing, still using the same eight-cylinder supercharged cars. They had little or no trouble in winning the first race of the 1950 season, which rather indicated that their withdrawal from racing during 1949 had not lost them very much. Their chief rivals were still Ferrari and Maserati, and while the former were going from strength to strength, the latter was beginning to fall by the wayside. The Ferrari racing team was now highly organized, with efficient workshops and an excellent design department and throughout the year a constant stream of experiment and design eminated from the Maranello factory. It had been hoped that the long-chassis, two-stage supercharged, four overhead camshaft, vee 12-cylinder Ferrari would be more than a match for the Alfa Romeos when they returned to racing, but the very first race proved that this was not to be the case.

Alfa Romeo was concentrating on more and more supercharge pressure with a continual increase in r.p.m. on the 158 engine, and they were producing a seemingly never-ending increase in power, the chassis and suspension being virtually unchanged since the inception of the car way back in 1938. With this continual rise in power output from this remarkable little 1500cc eight-cylinder engine, the fuel consumption was naturally getting worse. Consequently, the car had to carry enormous quantities of fuel in a large tail tank and pannier tanks on each side of the driving compartment—yet still they had to stop and refuel half way through a full-length Grand Prix. Ferrari was beginning to find that his highly supercharged 1½-litre was going the same way, and as Alfa Romeo had many years start on him in developing a given engine, he had some quiet thoughts with his new engineer, Aurelio Lampredi.

Running concurrently with the Formula for Grand Prix racing was a second Formula for cars of 2-litres capacity without superchargers, this being known as Formula 2, and short races for these

Alfa Romeo Type 158 supercharged 8 cylinder Grand Prix car of 1946-51

cars were being held as "curtain raisers" before the big Grand Prix events. The French, British and Germans were taking part in these races, with comparatively simple cars built around "semi-stock" components, such teams as Simca-Gordini, H.W.M., Connaught, and A.F.M. being the major contestants.

Ferrari had had quite a lot of experience with unsupercharged 2-litre engines in his earlier sports cars, so that it was not long before he joined Formula 2 with a single-seater car based on his sports V-12 engine. Throughout 1950 the Maranello firm carried out a remarkable program of development in Formula 1 and Formula 2, the smaller and lower powered cars doing much experimental work that was passed on to the faster Grand Prix machines. Having seen that development of the highly supercharged 1½-litre cars was getting out of hand—both as regards cost and complication—Ferrari dropped the design completely and began some remarkably quick development work on a new series of Grand Prix cars. The Lago-Talbots had shown that a slower car than the Alfa Romeos that could go through a race non-stop was not far behind at the finish, after the very fast cars had stopped to refuel and change tires. So Ferrari thought that if he could make

36

a large unsupercharged car that was nearly as fast as the Alfa Romeos, yet economical, he would have a greater chance of beating them than if he carried on with his complicated supercharged design, which, no matter what happened, was inevitably behind the 158 Alfa Romeo in development.

The 1½-litre Supercharged Ferrari

Although Ferrari had built sports cars for quite a time, and also raced them stripped of road equipment in "voiturette races" in 1947, it was not until the end of 1948 that the first pure Grand Prix Ferrari appeared. It was a very small and short single-seater fitted with a supercharged 60° V-12 cylinder engine of the same basic design as the sports car unit with a bore and stroke of 55x52.5 mm and using a 5-speed gearbox mounted on the rear of the engine. The chassis frame was made of two large diameter tubes, and suspension was independent to all four wheels—by double-wishbones and a transverse leaf spring at the front and by swing axles and transverse leaf spring at the rear. The engines did not develop a great deal of power, only about 230 b.h.p. at 7000 r.p.m.,

1950 supercharged two-stage 1500cc four camshaft 12 cylinder Ferrari Grand Prix Car

but the smallness of the whole car kept the overall weight down and the power-to-weight ratio was very favorable.

The first appearance of these new Grand Prix Ferraris was in the Italian Grand Prix at Turin in 1948. Three cars were entered, driven by Farina, Sommer and Bira, and the second of the three managed to get his new car on the front row of the starting grid. In this very first race the Ferrari showed that it was a match for the Maserati and the 158 Alfa Romeo, and Sommer ran in second place for quite a while, battling with Villoresi on a factory Maserati, and not too far behind Wimille on the leading Alfa Romeo. Sommer kept his car going for the whole 223 miles of the race and finished in third spot, only a few lengths behind the Maserati. The other two Ferraris retired, one with transmission trouble and the other due to a crash, but this first race for the new cars demonstrated clearly that the name Ferrari was going to be a powerful force in Grand Prix racing.

Just before the end of the 1948 season two cars ran in the Monza Grand Prix, driven by Farina and Sommer, and while they were going they were well in the thick of the battle, but Sommer was taken ill and had to retire, and Farina suffered from a transmission breakage. Their final outing that year was at Barcelona, where once more three cars were entered—in the hands of Farina, Bira and a local Spanish driver—but though Bira led the race for a time, all three were forced to retire with mechanical trouble.

In 1949 one of the original cars was sold to Peter Whitehead, the English driver, and another, as previously mentioned, to G. A. Vandervell. New cars were built for the factory with revised rear suspension, with the transverse leaf spring mounted above the axle assembly instead of below, the wheels supported on swinging half axles and still of only 85-inch wheelbase. With Alfa Romeo retired from racing these new Ferraris had only Maserati to beat, and this they did in the Swiss Grand Prix, the Dutch Grand Prix, and the Daily Express Silverstone race. They were beaten in other events for, though they were fast, their handling was not perfect due to a rather short wheelbase, and the engine design did not leave much room for development. Ascari and Villoresi formed the mainstay of the team, and were later joined by Cortese, and when a new model was introduced right at the end of the season, Sommer and Bonetto took over the earlier cars.

Being limited on power output with the single overhead camshaft layout on each bank of cylinders, it was decided to build an entirely new engine, still using the 60 degree V-12 construction, with the same over-square cylinder dimensions, but having two overhead camshafts to each bank, and two-stage supercharging by two Roots-type blowers mounted one above the other in front of the engine. This unit was fitted into a new chassis that was six inches longer in the wheelbase than the original Grand Prix Ferrari, and the suspension and brakes were greatly improved.

Two of these new long chassis cars were completed in time for the Grand Prix of Europe held at Monza and were driven by Ascari and Villoresi; the former led the race from start to finish, while the latter retired with gearbox trouble. The new engine was obviously far more powerful than any previous Ferrari engine, and the longer wheelbase and improved suspension changed the road-holding beyond all recognition. However, though Ascari won the race with ease, his speed was not as high as that of the winning Alfa Romeo in 1948, so that the following season, when Alfa Romeo returned to racing, this new two-stage 1½-litre 12-cylinder Ferrari met some strong opposition.

With interest beginning in the Formula 2 category and its un-supercharged 2-litre cars, Ferrari did not put as much effort into his two-stage supercharged cars as he might have done, but he forsaw that developing this new engine to the high state that Alfa Romeo had developed their 158 model was going to prove a very costly business. Ascari and Villoresi remained with the Scuderia Ferrari for 1950 and drove the two-stage cars at San Remo, but were soundly beaten by a lone Alfa Romeo. They ran again at Monaco, and once more could only finish second, and then at the Swiss Grand Prix one of the engines was fitted into a new chassis, with a 94-inch wheelbase developed for Formula 2, which had a de Dion rear suspension and a 4-speed gearbox integral with the axle, and much improved road holding.

Villoresi drove this car, while Ascari had one of the swing-axle cars, but both retired very early in the race, the former with a broken axle and the latter with a broken oil pipe. At the next event, the Belgian Grand Prix, only the swing-axle car was entered, for Ferrari was now beginning development of a large unsupercharged car for Grand Prix racing. The best that Ascari could do on the fast Spa circuit was 5th, and as Villoresi was just behind him in the experimental unsupercharged car, this finally decided Ferrari to drop the 1½-litre supercharged model. The swing-axle works car made one more appearance, at Silverstone, when it was lent to Mr. Vandervell for the B.R.D.C. meeting, but even though driven by Ascari it did not make any impression, and that saw the end of Ferrari's supercharged era.

Meanwhile, Peter Whitehead had been having numerous successes in small races with his old 1948 car, and Sommer also drove one of these in lesser events, as did Roberto Vallone and Dorino Serafini, the latter making up the works team until the big unblown cars were ready.

The Big Unblown Ferrari

The performance Ferrari was getting from his Formula 2 engine of only 2-litres unsupercharged encouraged him in the idea of a big unblown engine, and early in 1950 he had a new chassis that was proving successful in Formula 2 racing, so he began the development of a 4½-litre car on the same lines. The new chassis had a 94-inch wheelbase, still with double-wishbone and a transverse leaf spring independent front suspension, but in place of the swing-axle rear suspension he now used a de Dion layout in which the two wheels were joined together by a large diameter tube curving round the back of the differential unit, and located in a vertical slide at its center point. The wheel hubs were positioned fore and aft by two radius rods pivoted to give a parallelogram motion to the wheel in the vertical plane. The final drive unit was fixed rigidly to the chassis frame and universally jointed half-shafts took the drive out to the wheels.

The chassis frame itself consisted of two large-diameter tubular side members with tubular cross members, and a superstructure of smaller tubing was welded to the chassis to carry the body panels, tank and scuttle. With a slightly shorter wheelbase this layout first appeared with an unsupercharged 2-litre V-12 engine basically the same as that used in the Ferrari sports cars, with single overhead camshafts to each bank of cylinders, chain driven from the front of the crankshaft, the inclined valves being operated by rockers.

Halfway through the 1950 season the old long chassis car was run with the team of supercharged cars using a 3.3 litre unsupercharged V-12 cylinder engine, and then a little while later this interim engine was fitted into the new long chassis with de Dion suspension, and two such cars were built. On their very first appearance they seriously challenged the Alfa Romeos, making second and third fastest lap times in practice, whereas almost without exception Alfa Romeos figured to have all three of their cars in the front row of the start. Although neither of the new Ferraris finished this race, they made a serious challenge to the Alfa Romeo team and it was very clear that Ferrari had started on a sound line of development, for the cars were very fast even with only 3.3-litre engines. Before the end of the season 4½-litre engines were built and installed in the new chassis, the layout of these engines being identical with all Ferrari 12-cylinder units, having single overhead camshafts on each bank of cylinders, and three downdraft double-choke carburetors mounted in the vee of the engine.

This big Ferrari was a really serious challenge to Alfa Romeo supremacy, for not only was it as fast as the 158 Alfa Romeo but it had no need to stop for refuelling during a race, and it caused the Milan firm to bring out a much modified car, designated the *Tipo* 159. This car had much improved brakes and suspension, though the layout of trailing arms at the front and swing-axles at the rear remained the same, and the engine was now developing some 360 b.h.p. at 8500 r.p.m. Although the Alfa Romeo team continued to win every race for which they entered, the days of a 1-2-3 finishing order were over, for the new Ferrari was now right behind them, and at their last battle in 1950 it would have been a certain winner had it kept going.

41

The 1950 Ferrari 12 cylinder 4500cc unsupercharged Grand Prix car

With this keen battle waging between the two powerful Italian teams, Maserati got left behind. They were still racing the 4CLT/48, further developed but now very much behind in the b.h.p. race, and it looked as if the four-cylinder engine had reached the limits of its reliability. Of all the promising new designs that should have appeared during 1950, only the B.R.M. came to the starting line. Though it obviously developed enormous power from its supercharged 16-cylinder engine, it was far from ready to race and suffered so many troubles throughout the season that it could never be considered a serious challenge to either Alfa Romeo or Ferrari. The interesting and complicated Cisitalia was never completed, the firm going bankrupt before they ever raced the car, and the French C.T.A.-Arsenal project was abandoned. The Alta raced in the smaller meetings, but it was no match for the Italian cars. The rather large and cumbersome Lago-Talbots continued to support racing, being basically unchanged in design, but they also were no match for the Italians, being very underpowered in comparison with the 4½-litre Ferrari.

As most of the Grand Prix cars belonged to factory teams, the private-owner who wanted to race was limited to Lago-Talbot or Maserati, unless he wanted to try his luck with such cars as the

Alta or the already-out-dated Ferraris which the Maranello team had stopped driving. The new 4½-litre Ferraris and the 158 and 159 Alfa Romeos were definitely not for sale, nor was the B.R.M. In consequence, many of the amateur racing drivers were turning to the Formula 2 category, and these unsupercharged 2-litre cars were being built by many small firms and development was progressing rapidly.

The 4½-litre Lago-Talbot

In 1936, when France renounced Grand Prix racing and held most of her classic events for sports cars, the Talbot concern started racing again with large 4-litre 6-cylinder sports models, and in the following years they made occasional sorties into Grand Prix racing with these sports cars stripped of their road equipment. In 1939 they built a pure single-seater racing car, very much on the lines of the sports cars, especially as regards chassis and suspension. After the war this car formed the nucleus of the activities of the Talbot concern, headed by Anthony Lago, and in 1948 they constructed a number of new cars which had 4½-litre 6-cylinder engines. Although the factory sponsored entries themselves, the main aim was to build and sell these racing cars, which compiled with the 1947 Formula, and if required, to service the cars at the factory.

The 6-cylinder engine had a bore and stroke of 93 mm x 110 mm with total capacity of 4482 cc and had overhead valves inclined at an included angle of 95 degrees. They were operated by two camshafts mounted high in the cylinder block, with short pushrods and rockers, and the spark plugs were set in the center of the cylinder head. Carburetion was by three downdraft instruments and though the engine did not develop as much power as its supercharged rivals, it was remarkably reliable and also very economical so that the car could run a full length 300 mile Grand Prix without refueling.

Behind the engine was a 4-speed-and-reverse Wilson pre-selector gearbox and behind that a gear drive stepped the line of the transmission sideways to the right, so that the propellor shaft ran alongside the driving seat and allowed the driver to sit very low in the car. The rear axle was a conventional one-piece affair sprung on half-elliptic leaf springs, and the differential unit was offset from the center to line up with the propellor shaft. Front suspension was by a transverse leaf spring mounted under the chassis and attached to the bottom of the king posts, while a solid wishbone member pivoted on the chassis frame and was connected to the top of the king post. The chassis frame itself was a rather heavy structure of channel steel with tubular cross members.

During 1948 six of these cars were built and were driven by Louis Rosier, Pierre Levegh, Gianfranco Comotti, Louis Chiron, Philippe Etancelin, and "Raph." This first season did not see the Lago-Talbots do anything startling, but they were usually in at the finish, filling 3rd or 4th places by sheer consistent running. The following year Rosier won the Belgian Grand Prix and Chiron the French Frand Prix, by reason of these "tortoise and hare" principles, and there were numerous occasions on which they finished in quite high places. More new cars were built in 1949 and Guy Mairesse, George Grignard, Yves Giraud-Cabantous and Johnny Claes joined the Lago-Talbot ranks, while Raymond Sommer drove a factory sponsored car, as did Farina on one occasion.

There were no major changes carried out during the 1949 season, the factory concentrating on completing orders and looking after the customers' cars, though some experiments were made with dual ignition. The design of a new 16-cylinder supercharged engine to fit into the chassis was begun, but unfortunately never finished for, like so many racing factories, money was limited even though ideas were not. For the 1950 season the dual ignition cylinder head became standard and was fitted to most of the cars, while stronger crankshafts and improved cylinder blocks were fitted and horizontal Zenith carburetors replaced the original downdraft Solex carburetors.

The engine dimensions were unchanged, and in consequence of the long stroke, engine r.p.m. were limited to 5000 and at this figure the improved engines gave nearly 280 b.h.p. Two of the factory cars were rebuilt using all the new improvements and driven by Rosier and Giraud-Cabantous, while Harry Schell took over Rosier's 1949 car. Along with the other private-owners, they continued to worry the supercharged opposition by continually running through races non-stop and gaining time while their rivals were at the pits refueling and fitting new tires. Rosier continued to be the most successful of the Lago-Talbot drivers and during 1950 he won the Dutch Grand Prix and the Pescara Grand Prix, in which race he was timed over a kilometre at 166 m.p.h.

Altogether, four 1950 cars were run by the factory—driven by Rosier, Cabantous, Etancelin and Sommer—but by the end of the season they were beginning to be outclassed by the new 4½-litre Ferrari which was not only playing the same game, of running through the races non-stop, but was also proving as fast as the supercharged cars. The Talbot-Darracq firm was by now getting into financial difficulties, for though their racing program was supposed to be assisting the development and production of passenger cars, there was little or no market for the large 4½-litre road cars, and in 1951 the situation became so difficult that the factory had to give up all racing activity.

However, Louis Rosier financed a team of cars using the 1950 models and continued to keep the name of Lago-Talbot in Grand Prix racing, but by now there was little hope of success for the furious pace of the Alfa Romeo and Ferrari teams had left the French cars too far behind even for "tortoise and hare" tactics to pay off. In the smaller events which were not supported by the big factories, the Lago-Talbots were still able to give their owners some good racing, while one of the 1949 cars was bought by Duncan-Hamilton and with it he enlivened the British racing scene with some furious driving. But in major Grand Prix racing, the 1951 season saw the virtual disappearance of the Lago-Talbots. Since 1948 they had persevered but always seemed to be one year behind their rivals in development, although had Anthony Lago got the new design going in 1947 at the very beginning of the postwar Formula the cars might have achieved more success than they did. As it was they only just managed to keep the French colors in racing, with occasional victories due to the misfortunes of their rivals.

Throughout their life of development they did not alter greatly, retaining the same engine dimensions all the time, using the Wilson pre-selector gearbox, never changing the chassis, retaining the wheelbase of 98½ inches, a front track of 54 inches and a rear track of 51½ inches. And they had kept the same suspension system as was built onto the original 1939 prototype.

With European racing changing over to small unsupercharged 2-litre cars in 1952 the Lago-Talbots all retired from racing, except for very minor meetings in France and England, and one or two of the cars were converted into two-seater sports cars. Some drivers, such as Etancelin and Rosier, put their cars into the corner of a garage and covered them over and let them go into honorable retirement, a fond memory of a past age.

While the Grand Prix cars were having a horsepower race, with high supercharge pressures vying against sheer cylinder capacity, the Formular 2 designers were spending a great deal of time on the development of chassis and suspension design, being limited as to power output.

The 1950 season finished on a very high note, for Alfa Romeo won the penultimate Grand Prix due to the Ferrari being unreliable, and Ferrari won the final race, having achieved reliability, but mainly because Alfa Romeo did not enter. The result was that the question of which limit of the Grand Prix Formula was best, the supercharged 1½-litre engine or the unsupercharged 4½-litre engine, was still wide open.

This was a remarkable period in Grand Prix racing design, for when the 1950 season began no one would have refuted the fact that the supercharged 1½-litre, as exemplified by Alfa Romeo, was supreme. In one short season Ferrari had not only put doubts in everyone's mind but had more or less proved, even though he had not yet won a race, that an unsupercharged 4½-litre was equal, if not superior, to anything on the road. It was the first time that any designer had made a really serious attempt at a big unsupercharged Grand Prix car, the Talbot being a compromise from sports car racing, so it was not altogether surprising. And it was a complete justification of the Formula as laid down in 1947.

5. UNSUPERCHARGED 1½ LITRE vs. SUPERCHARGED 4½ LITRE

By F.I.A. rules the Grand Prix Formula should have been changed in 1950, but it had been agreed to leave things as they were for racing was proving interesting and design and development work was going on apace. The aims of the technical commission of the F.I.A. which decides the rules for a Grand Prix Formula are to encourage the development and design of racing cars, and to this end the rules are changed if there is a distinct sign of stagnation setting in, or if the line of development being taken by the manufacturers is heading in what is considered to be the wrong direction as regards logical design work. With the 1½-litre and 4½-litre Formulae at last showing equality there was no interest in making a change, and the Formula remained in being for a further three years—throughout 1951-52 and '53—but at the same time the Formula 2 category was kept going.

Once again the season opened full of promise, and whereas 1950 had been a good season, but unpredictable at the beginning, the 1951 season went according to plan. Ferrari was in the ascendant, having a sound design that was showing great promise, Alfa Romeo had got their development program so organized that the 159 cars were going better than ever before, and B.R.M. had a good design that was getting under way. The supporting cast would be made up by Maserati, now rather out of the picture, Alta, who were still struggling along, and Lago-Talbot, while Gordini had added a supercharger to his little 1500 cc "voiturettes" and was also joining in Grand Prix racing.

In Bologna the Maserati brothers, who had left the concern that was still using their name, were building a new Formula 1 car at their new factory, known as the *Officine Specializate Costruzione Automobili*, or Osca for short. This was a V-12 cylinder engined car of 4½ litres capacity; at first the engine was installed in a modified 4CLT Maserati chassis, later in a new OSCA chassis. This car had great promise but came to nothing, due to OSCA being financially unable to develop the car quick enough to keep up with the pace being set by Alfa Romeo and Ferrari.

The expected battles between Alfa Romeo and Ferrari came up to all expectations, and the Milan firm fielded a team of four cars in their efforts to prevent Ferrari winning, while they brought out a new version of the 159 which they used in practice at first. The remarkable straight-eight engine was still basically unchanged, and surprisingly kept the same bore and stroke as it had used in the very early days, power output being put up by continual increases of supercharger pressure. This was obtained by putting up the r.p.m. and increasing the size of the Roots blowers and the special three-choke Weber carburetor used on these engines. They were now running at 9000 r.p.m. and giving nearly 400 b.h.p., but at the cost of astronomical fuel consumption and not very good reliability. For everything in the engine was working right on the limits of safety, and the slightest error of adjustment of carburetion, spark plugs or fuel meant a wrecked engine, while a heavy footed driver could very easily do a lot of damage in a short time.

As the season progressed the Alfa Romeo team was racing against the inevitable, which was defeat by Ferrari, and the racing was so fast and furious that there was no possibility of bringing out a new design. They had no choice but to go on with the straight-eight, it having got into an uncontrollable flight of high pressure development. Since 1938 the Alfa Romeo had been content to use swing-axle rear suspension, but now that the pressure was on they had to try and find more speed from the chassis as well as the engine, and the experimental car that appeared at the beginning of the season had a de Dion rear axle layout. Although the Alfa Romeos won the first three important races of 1951 they were very shaky wins, and in the first a Ferrari was second, in the next race Ferraris were 2nd and 3rd, and in the third race unsupercharged Ferraris finished 2nd, 3rd and 4th.

So it was a very uneasy Alfa Romeo team that arrived at the next big race. The 4½-litre Ferraris were getting stronger and stronger all the time, with improvements to road holding and braking, and with engines developing nearly as much power as their supercharged rivals, now using duel ignition cylinder heads, but otherwise unchanged from the original 12-cylinder layout. With the Alfa Romeo team really on the run, it was just a matter of time before they were caught, and when they were, at the British Grand Prix, there took place one of the greatest motor races of all time. An homeric battle was waged between those two great drivers Fangio and Gonzalez, the former doing all he knew to defend the honour of Alfa Romeo while the latter was driving with a mad abandon spurred on by the knowledge that he had at last got the "invincible" Alfa Romeos on the run. Until this memorable day the supercharged straight-eights had never been beaten, but this time, though they fought grimly, they still had to take 2nd place.

In barely 12 months Ferrari had vanquished his rivals with an entirely new design and had proven the Formula to be a reasonable one, and after this first victory he went on to greater things. Meanwhile the Alfa Romeo team went all to pieces, for the strain of being kept on the run at such a pace had taken its toll, and at the next race they were again beaten, collecting 2nd place again, but this time without the same fight.

They had reached a desperate situation, for not only had they met their match, but their cars were anything but reliable now, being much too highly tuned for safety. And they had no advantages in road holding, in spite of the de Dion axle layout on two of the cars, for Ferrari was just as far ahead in the chassis design race. The two giants of racing met again in a minor race and this time Alfa Romeo had a victory, but confidence was short lived, for there followed the Italian Grand Prix on their home ground and here they were thoroughly beaten by the Ferraris, only one out of four Alfa Romeos finishing the race.

Ferrari was becoming more and more confident and after his

three magnificent victories everyone expected yet another at the
final race of the year in Spain, but he made an error with tire
dimensions and his cars had to keep stopping for new covers, so
that Alfa Romeo was able to hang on for one more win. For this
race both teams had fielded four cars, all the Alfa Romeos being
the latest de Dion suspension models, and the Ferraris all being
24 plug 12 cylinder 4½ litres.

Not for many years had Grand Prix racing been at such an interesting stage, for the two major teams were so even in performance, road holding, drivers, and organization that results depended
on one of the other making a mistake in some trifling detail. The
pace set by these two teams had been so great that the rest of the
Grand Prix constructors had been left far behind, Maserati now
being completely out of the picture, the Osca being unable to keep
up the pace of development, and Lago-Talbot an also-ran. The
B.R.M. had begun to make its appearance, and though technically the equal of the two Italian teams it suffered from inex-
perienced management and was never a serious challenge. In support of the factory Ferrari team was the "Thinwall Special"—that

The 4500cc Ferrari as modified by the Vandervell racing team and driven by Farina

50

privately owned 4½-litre Ferrari run by G. A. Vandervell. It was being modified and developed in England and though not the equal of the works cars, it was a good runner-up and provided additional opposition to the supercharged cars.

The Type 4C Maserati

During the mid-thirties the Maserati brothers were taking part in all types of racing, including Grand Prix, voiturette and sports car events, building a variety of models both for their own factory team and for sale to private owners. With Grand Prix racing development progressing at an alarming and expensive rate from 1934 to 1939, Maserati concentrated more on voiturette racing, which was for 1½-litre cars with superchargers. After a successful run with a six cylinder car that was advanced for its day in having independent front suspension, hydraulic braking system, and the use of elektron in many of the components, they designed and built an entirely new car for the 1939 season.

This was the Type 4C and had a twin-overhead camshaft 4-cylinder engine of square bore and stroke dimensions, these being 78 x 78 mm giving a capacity of 1494 cc. There were four valves to each cylinder, two inlet and two exhaust, and a Roots-type supercharger was mounted on the front of the crankcase. This car soon became known as the "16 valve Maserati" and developed its power at 8000 r.p.m., these crankshaft speeds being attainable by reason of the very short stroke employed for those far off days. A four-speed gearbox was fitted to the engine and this drove via an open propellor shaft to a conventional rear axle which was mounted on ¼-elliptic springs with radius arms alongside them to take the torque of braking and accelerating. Front suspension was independent, as used on the earlier 6-cylinder cars, having double wishbone members with the top ones coupled to longitudinal torsion bars. Each wheel had its own steering arm and drag link, there being a drop arm from each end of the steering box spindle, which was itself split in the center and had reverse direction worm mechanism in the steering box. The engine was dry-sump, and there was an elektron oil tank under the driving seat which formed a very sturdy cross-member for the channel section chassis frame.

During 1939 the 4C was developed, and though it proved faster than the 158 Alfa Romeo, which was its chief rival, it was less reliable. By the end of the season it was finally getting over its teething troubles, but then the war started and put the end to motor racing. In 1939 the factory team consisted of Luigi Villoresi, Count Trossi and Franco Cortese; a number of private owners bought these new models, among them the two British drivers Reggie Tongue and John Wakefield and the Swiss driver Armand Hug, all of them being most satisfied with the cars. As an interim model, one or two cars were built using the older six-cylinder type of chassis fitted out with the 1939 four cylinder engine and gearbox.

After the war the Maserati firm continued to race a team of 16-valve cars, working in close co-operation with private owners, and these cars formed the mainstay of racing in 1946 and 1947, there quite often being small races in Italy and France that consisted of a field entirely composed of 4C Maseratis. Among the drivers who were active with these cars in the immediate post-war period, either using 1939 models or new ones, were B.Bira, Reg Parnell, Roy Salvadori, David Murray, Baron de Graffenried, Raymond Sommer and Luigi Villoresi.

Naturally the factory continued to develop the 16-valve car, and one of the first modifications to be made was the addition of another supercharger, this being mounted above the original one in front of the engine, and they were coupled in series; the lower one, or first-stage, blowing into the upper one or second-stage, and thence to the inlet manifold. Another major development was the fitting of a tubular chassis frame in place of the original channel-section frame.

After two successful seasons the 4C and its later development, 4CL, were discontinued and the 4 CLT/48 car was designed, being not entirely new but a major development of the original car. It was at this point that the Maserati brothers sold their firm to the Omar Orsi, a rich industrialist of Modena, and formed the new firm named Osca. The Orsi family continued the Maserati development program, designing the 4 CLT/48 car, and continued to support racing by running a works team and offering facilities to private owners, still retaining the name Maserati and continuing the factory in Modena.

The 4 CLT/48 Maserati

Using the same 4-cylinder engine, with two-stage supercharging, and the same four-speed gearbox as the earlier 4CL cars, this new model differed mainly in having a new chassis frame and front suspension and being much lower than the previous model. The chassis was tubular and of the "ladder" formation, while the front suspension was still independent but of a new form. Double wishbones were employed, with the top one being extended inwards across the car beyond the pivot point, this extension bearing on the top of a coil spring, so that as the wheels rose over bumps the top wishbones, acting as rockers, compressed the coil springs. The chassis members were curved downwards from the front suspension and the engine and gearbox were mounted much lower in the chassis than on previous Maserati cars. To accommodate this lowering, the rear axle had a pair of step-up gears mounted on the nose of the differential housing. The rear axle was still a conventional one-piece layout and retained the $\frac{1}{4}$-elliptic springing.

Factory sponsored cars were driven during 1948 by Luigi Villoresi, long associated with the name Maserati, and by a new protége of his, Alberto Ascari, son of the famous driver of the early 1920's. A number of these new cars were sold to private owners, among them being Bira and Parnell. This new Maserati model made its first appearance at a small race on the Italian Riviera, at San Remo, and for this reason the 4 CLT/48 is often referred to as the "San Remo Maserati."

In 1949 Ascari and Villoresi joined the Ferrari team, and Maserati fortunes were upheld by an Argentinian team, working in close co-operation with the Modena factory, the drivers being

Juan Fangio and Benedicto Campos. Parnell still raced his car, and Bira and de Graffenried drove for an Italian private team, using the latest models. Later in the season Maserati entered a factory car driven by Farina, and, supported by the various private Scuderias, the name of Maserati figured frequently in the results and provided many stirring battles against the Ferrari team.

In 1950, with Alfa Romeo returning to racing, the 4 CLT/48 Maserati began to get outpaced in the bigger races, but they were still raced by private teams such as the Argentine Scuderia, Parnell's team and the Italian team run by Enrico Plate, while Louis Chiron and Franco Rol occasionally drove factory cars. However, the engine was becoming very unreliable, being too highly stressed and too highly supercharged, and by the end of the season they could not keep pace with the fantastic Alfa Romeos.

This season was the last really active one for Maserati cars of the 4-cylinder type and, though the factory made a few races in 1950, by the end of the year they had withdrawn completely and were only giving very small support to the last of the remaining private owners. Such cars that remained were sadly lacking in reliability so that the 4 CLT/48 Maserati as a model faded from the Grand Prix picture on a rather dismal note.

While this great battle was being waged between the supercharged 1½-litres and the unsupercharged 4½-litres, the Formula 2 was being supported strongly by many small firms, as well as by Ferrari. At the end of the 1951 season the F.I.A. announced that a new Formula for Grand Prix cars would begin in 1954 and would be for supercharged cars of 750cc and unsupercharged cars of 2500cc, or in other words a mixture of the two existing Formulae. With this announcement it was not surprising that Alfa Romeo decided to withdraw from racing once again, for their 159 cars had reached their limit of development and they could only continue to battle against Ferrari in a very unreliable and delicate condition.

There was not time to design a new car for the 1952 season, and with the existing Formula being valid for only 1952 and 1953 there was no justification for starting on a new design of super-charged 1½-litre. The Milan technicians were well aware that the 4½-litre Ferrari was not at the end of its development, and that their cars were at the end of a most successful run. In all the post war years of racing they had been beaten but three times, and all three were at the latter end of the 1951 season, so they graciously withdrew from Grand Prix racing and the phenomenal little *Tipo* 159 cars were put away never to race again.

In passing it is interesting to note that these cars first raced in 1938 and underwent development from then until the end of 1951, during which time the power output of the engine rose from 195 h.b.p. to an all time high in experimental form of 410 b.h.p. without any change in bore and stroke or capacity. Superchargers went from one quite small Roots instrument to a gigantic two-stage Roots layout, and Alfa Romeo probably learned more about supercharging and its problems than anyone else during those memorable years. Of the complete team only three cars were retained, for museum purposes, the other being broken up, and none were ever sold outside the factory.

However, the engines were later used in racing hydroplanes and only recently, in 1958, the last of the 159 Alfa Romeo engines was lost when a racing boat sunk off the coast of Florida. There now remains only one working 159 engine and that is in a car in Alfa Romeo's own museum, but it is a tribute to one of the finest Grand Prix cars of all time, with a record of success that is hard to beat.

The Alfa Romeo Type 158

First built in 1938, the little 8-cylinder supercharged 1½-litre Alfa Romeos represented scaled-down versions of the Grand Prix cars that were current at that time. Three cars were entered for the Coppa Ciano, their very first race, and two of them finished 1st and 2nd. In a later race that year a timed speed for a flying kilometre of 141 m.p.h. was achieved. In 1939 they created a sensation at the Swiss Grand Prix when Dr. Guiseppe Farina lay 2nd for quite a time, behind a 3-litre Mercedes-Benz and ahead of all the other Mercedes-Benz and Auto-Union cars. He eventually finished a very honorable 6th, ahead of four of the bigger cars. In 1940 four of these cars were entered for the Tripoli Grand Prix and finished 1st, 2nd and 3rd. Farina was once more the winner, averaging 128 m.p.h. with a fastest lap of over 132 m.p.h.

After the war the cars were rebuilt and modified in detail, and the Alfa Romeo factory sponsored a team of four cars with Farina, Trossi, Wimille and Varzi, all pre-war racing drivers of great repute. The biggest change since 1940 was the adoption of two-stage supercharging to the eight-cylinder engine, though the bore and stroke remained unchanged at 58 mm x 70 mm.

In 1947 Farina left the team and his place was taken by Consalvo Sanesi, one of the factory test-drivers, and in 1948 they lost Varzi, who was killed while practicing with an experimental car. Newcomers to the team were Alberto Ascari and Piero Taruffi, and by the end of the season three of the new models were being raced, finishing 1-2-3 in the Monza Grand Prix, with an older model in 4th place. These new cars had a higher degree of supercharging, and new exhaust manifolding with all eight cylinders discharging into one tail pipe, whereas previously they had used two tailpipes, one serving each set of four cylinders. Suspension was still by two trailing arms to each front wheel and a transverse leaf spring between them, and at the rear swing axles were used with forward running radius arms and a transverse leaf spring mounted very low behind the assembly. The chassis frame was made of oval section tubing, and hydraulic brakes with large diameter finned drums were used.

In 1949 Alfa Romeo withdrew from racing to concentrate on building up their production of passenger cars, and the 158 team of cars were put away in a corner of the racing department. In spite of many offers the cars were not sold or loaned to anyone and remained silent throughout the season. During this recession Wimille was killed while driving another make of car in South America and Felice Trossi died of illness, so that Alfa Romeo were probably very glad that they had stopped racing.

In 1950 the cars reappeared again and for the first race a car was given to Juan Fangio. He won with ease. For the rest of the season Farina rejoined the team, and a veteran driver, one Luigi Fagioli, was signed on. During the year they competed in eleven races, and one or the other of the drivers finished first in all eleven events. At the end of the season Taruffi was taken on again, to make up a four car team, and in England, where they finished 1-2-3 at Silverstone, Reg Parnell was loaned a car. In Switzerland Baron de Graffenried made up the fourth place in the team, for his own National Grand Prix. For their last race of the season five cars were entered, this being the Italian Grand Prix at Monza, and the drivers were Fangio, Farina, Fagioli, Taruffi and Sanesi. Fangio and Farina had new cars with an improved braking system, larger and more powerful drum brakes, and a much higher power output—360 b.h.p. agianst the 158A's 340 b.h.p.

However, these new engines were getting very fragile and, though fast, were not 100% reliable. At Pescari in 1950 one of the cars was timed over the flying kilometre at 195 m.p.h.—an increase of more than 50 m.p.h. over the same distance in 1938. The Drivers World Championship was introduced in 1950 and Farina was the winner, driving for Alfa Romeo with the 158 and 159 models.

In 1951 the Alfa Romeo team consisted of Farina, Fangio, Sanesi and a newcomer, Felice Bonetto, while in the Swiss Grand Prix de Graffenried once more was loaned a car, and in the German Grand Prix Paul Pietsch took the spare car. Although they still won races, victory was no longer a certainty. The opposition from Ferrari was strong, and during the season the Alfa Romeo team were defeated on three occasions. However, they were able to win enough races for Fangio to take the World Championship title.

During the season they experimented with a new car fitted with a de Dion rear axle layout, though still using a transverse leaf spring, while the rest of the car remained unchanged, except for reverting to dual exhaust pipes again, and of course, engine development continued. This final version of the 159 Alfa Romeo still had the 58 x 70 mm bore and stroke, used two Roots super-chargers in series, with an enourmous triple choke Weber carburetor, and developed nearly 400 b.h.p. at 9000 r.p.m. Throughout the wheelbase stayed at 98 inches and the track at 49 inches, the front track later in their life being increased to 53 inches.

Alfa Romeo racing ceased altogether at the end of 1951, with the 159 cars at the highest pitch of tune imaginable, but they ended their glorious history of racing and development from 1938 to 1951 by finishing 1st, 3rd, 5th and 6th in the Spanish Grand Prix, the drivers being Fangio, Farina, Bonetto and Graffenried. In all the years of post-war racing they suffered only three defeats, all at the hands of Ferrari, and they provided the car for the first two World Champions in the series of contests that began in 1950.

As recorded, with the change of Formula for Grand Prix racing envisaged for 1954, the Alfa Romeo racing department closed its doors and the 158 and 159 Alfa Romeos were mostly dismantled, though three were retained for Museum purposes—one de Dion 159 and a 158 being kept at the Milan factory and one 158 model being put in the Turin Automobile Museum—while all the spare engines were subsequently used . . . speedboat racing.

6. FORMULA 2 COMES TO STAY

With Alfa Romeo now out of racing, the 1952 season was left wide open for Ferrari and his unsupercharged 4½-litre cars, though it was hoped that B.R.M. would take the place of the Milan firm. When the season began the scene was very unsettled and many race organizers were in favor of holding meetings for the small Formula 2 cars, for there was more likelihood of support among the growing band of small constructors, and Ferrari would be there anyway, no matter **what** Formula was adhered to.

The fate of the 1952 season really rested on the shoulders of the people at Bourne, for if the B.R.M. appeared and showed promise of providing opposition to Ferrari then Formula I would go on. As it turned out the B.R.M. was very tardy in starting the 1952 season and almost overnight, after one race had been run as a 4½-litre Ferrari benefit, all the major races switched to Formula 2 and the whole aspect of Grand Prix racing changed. From racing involving fantastic powers and speeds, from cars that could wear out their rear tires in a few hundred miles and use fuel at the rate of 3 or 4 m.p.g., in other words, blood and thunder racing, Grand Prix now became comparatively tame with the small unsupercharged 2-litre cars with a mere 150 b.h.p. available, so that pitstops for fuel and tires became a thing of the past and lap speeds dropped enormously.

Although nearly all the big races of 1952 were run to Formula 2 rules, the Formula 1 was still in existence and there was one race held for this category in France. It saw a clash between the 4½-litre Ferraris and the B.R.M., but the British team was most unreliable and the whole of the continent turned to Formula 2 and it was only in Great Britain that Formula 1 was held. As this did not interest Ferrari, he preferring to race his Formula 2 cars, the

British races were left to B.R.M. However, they found quite enough opposition from the "Thinwall Special," the 4½-litre Ferrari that had been purchased by G. A. Vandervell. This car underwent many modifications to engine, chassis and brakes in the Vandervell workshops and in effect carried on Formula 1 activity in the place of the Ferrari factory. There were many stirring battles waged in small races all over Britain between the "Thinwall" and the B.R.M. team, but it was quite obvious that it was for a lost cause, as Formula 2 had obviously come to stay in European racing.

The Unsupercharged 4½-litre Ferrari

Unsupercharged multi-cylinder engines were nothing new to Enzo Ferrari and his engineers, for he had been developing his classic 60 degree V-12 engine for sports car racing in 1½-litre, 2-litre and 2.3-litre versions, and realizing the desirability of this type of unit for sports cars, he was quick to turn his experiments to Formula 1 when he saw the opportunity. As had been mentioned, the two-stage supercharged 1½-litre Grand Prix engine was a complicated and costly unit, having no connection with any other type of activity. Ferrari had always maintained that racing should have an end product, no matter how distant, and he could see that by following the unsupercharged field he could turn his experience to greater uses in production roadsters.

His first experiment in the Formula 1 field with an unsupercharged car was at the Belgian Grand Prix in 1950, when he built a 3.3-litre engine on exactly similar lines to his sports car unit and fitted it into one of the chassis that had previously held the supercharged 1½-litre unit. Villoresi drove the car, which came as a surprise to all concerned as Ferrari had kept very quiet about it, but it was soon rumored that he intended to go up to the full 4½-litre limit of the Formula. This experimental car proved virtually as fast as the supercharged Ferrari, so that even in this small capacity form the new Ferrari could be considered promising. Although the car practiced for the French Grand Prix it did not take part, as it was not considered to be ready for such a fast race, but in the next few weeks two new cars were built, using the 1950 chassis that had been developed in Formula II, with a four-speed gearbox in unit with the differential and a de Dion rear suspension.

These two cars were ready for the Swiss Grand Prix and were driven by Ascari and Villoresi, and though the engines were still only of 3.3-litre capacity, they were a match for the Alfa Romeo team. Ascari led at the start and only Fangio was able to catch him, after which he sat in 2nd position quite easily, while Villoresi ran in 5th place. With the race practically finished Villoresi had a bad crash and Ascari was robbed of a certain 2nd place by an engine failure. With Villoresi badly hurt and one car destroyed, the Scuderia Ferrari withdrew from racing for a time and concentrated on completing the new 4½-litre engines, and these were ready in September for the Italian Grand Prix on the fast Monza road circuit.

With Villoresi still unfit, the second car was driven by Dorino Serafini, both cars being the full capacity limit of the Grand Prix Formula and having the very latest chassis with de Dion rear suspension. From the start of the race Ascari sat right on the tail of the fastest and newest Alfa Romeo and all he had to do was to sit and wait, for the supercharged Alfa Romeo would have to make a pit stop for fuel at least once, and possibly twice in view of the hard pace that was being set. On sheer speed and acceleration the 4½-litre Ferrari was a comfortable match for the powerful Alfa Romeo and yet it could run the whole race distance on one tank full of fuel, the three double-choke downdraft carburetors on the V-12 engine being much more economical than the triple-choke carburetor and two-stage supercharging of the 1½-litre straight-eight. However, it was not to be, for after only a quarter of the race had been run the big Ferrari broke down, leaving the Alfa Romeo way out in the lead. The second Ferrari was in 6th place and it was brought in to the pits and Ascari took over from Serafini, and with no trouble at all he worked his way up to finish in 2nd place.

The development of the big unblown engine for Formula I had

never been seriously tackled before, the Lago-Talbot having no real development work done on it, and the experiments with the 3.3-litre Ferrari were so promising that it was no surprise to see that the 4½-litre car was a match for the all-conquering Alfa Romeos, though it had yet to find reliability enough to finish in first place. To conclude the 1950 season the Ferrari team competed in the Spanish Grand Prix, but Alfa Romeo did not enter this race so the big unblown cars had little opposition. The two 4½-litre cars were driven again by Ascari and Serafini, while Taruffi had one with a 4.1-litre engine, as used in Ferrari sports cars. It was a complete walk-over for them and they finished in 1-2-3 order, which must have worried Alfa Romeo for it showed that the Ferrari cars were gaining reliability.

As can be imagined, the 1951 season was looked forward to with great excitement, for it was now only a question of time before the all-conquering Alfa Romeo team met their match in open battle.

Ferrari started the season by using the 1950 cars, and in the smaller races had no difficulty in winning, as Alfa Romeo did not enter. Even so, the 4½-litres were not 100% reliable and twice Ascari had to retire while leading, but Villoresi was now back in the team and each time he stepped into the lead. For the race at San Remo the first of the 1951 cars was completed and driven by Ascari, while Villoresi and Serafini had the 1950 models. The new car was basically the same as the earlier models, but the engine had been redesigned, there now being two spark plugs per cylinder, one on the inside of the vee and the other on the outside in between the exhaust pipes. In places of the two six-cylinder magnetos on the old engines, there was a single aircraft type magneto which fired all 24 plugs.

In addition to these engine improvements and an increase in power output, new and larger brakes were built, having much more rigid drums and back plates. This new car won its first race with ease, Serafini being second, while poor Villoresi collided with another car and had to retire with a damaged radiator. At the B.R.D.C. Silverstone meeting there were no factory cars, but Mr.

Vandervell was there with his "Thinwall Special," which was driven by Reg Parnell.

For the Swiss Grand Prix a team of three 4½-litre Ferraris were entered, Ascari and Villoresi being joined by Taruffi, as Serafini had been injured in a sports car crash. Ascari and Taruffi drove the 1951 models and Villoresi had a 1950 car, fitted with the latest brakes but using a 12-plug engine. This race should have been the first real battle between the unblown Ferraris and the supercharged Alfa Romeos, no other makes being in the picture, but Ascari was still suffering from burns received in an earlier Formula II race and Villoresi ran off the road and bent his car, so it was left to Taruffi to show the paces of the big Ferraris. He drove extremely well to finish in 2nd place but Fangio dominated the race for Alfa Romeo.

In Britain the "Thinwall" Ferrari was making its mark, driven by Parnell, and among his exploits he set up a new lap record for the Goodwood circuit. At the Belgian Grand Prix the factory team had three 1951 cars, all with the latest 24-plug engines, developing 370 b.h.p. at 7500 r.p.m. They were driven by the same trio, Ascari, Villoresi and Taruffi. On the very fast Spa circuit the Alfa Romeos kept out in front, but Ascari finished 2nd and Villoresi 3rd, neither of them being very far behind the leader, while Taruffi had transmission trouble.

At the French Grand Prix which followed, Taruffi could not drive so his place was taken by Froilan Gonzalez, the Argentine driver. All three cars had been reworked in the body, the scuttle now having a smoother contour with a curved perspex screen moulded into it. Parnell drove the "Thinwall," so that Alfa Romeo was faced with really powerful opposition. Unfortunately Ascari went out with a broken gearbox early in the race, but he later took over from Gonzalez and finished second, Villoresi was third and Parnell fourth, but still victory was eluding the big Ferraris.

To finish 2nd, 3rd and 4th behind their rivals really meant that victory was only a matter of time, and it happened in the following race, the British Grand Prix at Silverstone. Ascari and Villoresi drove the new 24-plug cars and Gonzalez was on the earlier 12-plug model, and the Argentinian drove a race that was to become a classic. After making fastest practice time, beating all the Alfa Romeos, he fought a truly homeric battle with Fangio throughout the race and brought victory to the 4½-litre Ferrari by nearly one minute. Villoresi finished in 3rd place so that Alfa Romeo was really "on the run" and these big unblown cars had achieved this in a little over 12 months.

For the German Grand Prix which followed, Taruffi rejoined the team, making four cars in all, and they really trounced everyone on the Nurburgring, Ascari finishing 1st, Gonzalez 3rd, Villoresi 4th and Taruffi 5th. The Ferrari team was now truly confident that it was going to dominate Grand Prix racing, but a little later they had two setbacks, perhaps due to over-confidence. At Pescara, where Alfa Romeo did not enter and a Ferrari benefit seemed certain, although Gonzalez won, Ascari retired on the opening lap and then taking over Villoresi's car he went out with rear axle trouble. Two weeks later, at Bari, another shock was given them when Fangio led from start to finish in an Alfa Romeo, and though Gonzalez was 2nd, Ascari and Villoresi both had to retire.

The Scuderia Ferrari were now on their metal, and for the Italian Grand Prix at Monza, where the eyes of the motor racing world were on them, they fielded five cars. This race they just had to win, to convince Italy of who had the superior car, while Alfa Romeo was equally keen to win. Until now honors were about even between the two teams, so this 1951 Italian Grand Prix was one of the greatest "needle matches" of all time. Ascari, Villoresi and Gonzalez had the latest 1951 cars with 24-plug engines and head fairings behind the driver, Taruffi had an interim model having the new engine in an old chassis, and the Brazilian driver, Chico Landi had a 1950 model.

This powerful team really forced the pace, and though Landi broke his transmission, Ascari led the others on to a rousing victory, with Gonzalez 2nd, Villoresi 4th and Taruffi 5th, only one Alfa Romeo getting in the picture. To conclude this history-making season, the Ferrari team went to Barcelona for the Spanish Grand Prix, entering Ascari, Villoresi, Gonzales and Taruffi, but they made a tactical error in tire sizes and were delayed by throwing treads, so that in an air of confusion Gonzalez was lucky to finish 2nd and Ascari 4th. The other two both retired with mechanical trouble.

In 1952, with Alfa Romeo withdrawing, interest waned in Formula 1 racing and Ferrari was left with his powerful team of 4½-litre cars and nowhere to race them. After the speed shown at Monza the previous year, he decided to enter for Indianapolis and began preparing a team of cars for the 500-mile Memorial Day race. Early in the season he gave two of the "Indianapolis" cars a try-out in a small Italian race in Turin, with Ascari and Farina as drivers, while Villoresi had a 1951 car. This was an easy win for them, Villoresi being 1st, though the other two had trouble. Two of the older cars were sold to private owners—the Brazilian Landi and Frenchman Louis Rosier—and they competed in events in France and England, while the "Thinwall" Ferrari was still a regular competititor in the smaller events, now having English brakes, a new body and a 24-plug engine.

Ascari went to Indianapolis with one of the new cars, and three others were sent over for owners Jerry Grant, Johnny Mauro and Howard Keck, but of the four only the "works" car qualified, Ascari being in 19th position on the starting grid. The Ferrari was not really suited to the high-speed American track, and the best the great Italian driver could do was to get into 12th position, but then had to retire when a rear hub broke up.

The End of The 4½-Litre Ferrari

With Formula 1 racing practically finished in Europe, and Grand Prix events being run to Formula 2 specifications, there was little chance to race the big cars. But in England a special event was put on at Silverstone, and Ferrari sent Villoresi with one of the new cars and he was backed up by Landi and Rosier with their earlier models and Taruffi on the "Thinwall Special." It was a Ferrari benefit, the only opposition coming from B.R.M.—which did not last—and Taruffi was 1st, Villoresi 2nd and Landi 3rd. The "works" car made one more appearance, in England, at which Villoresi won. It was then returned to Italy and retirement, for there were no more suitable races for it. However, the "Thinwall Special" continued to race in English races, driven by Hawthorn and Farina, while Rosier also stayed on and raced his car.

1953 was the last year, officially, of the 4½-litre Formula, though organizers had already given up the big cars in favor of 2-litre cars, so there was no encouragement for Ferrari to develop his big cars any further. However, he did send one to Agentina for the winter races, more than anything else as a yardstick by which to measure the performance of his prototype car for the 1954 Formula. The only other time the factory 4½-litre appeared was for a race at Albi in France. With the factory concentrating on Formula 2 and the development of the new 2½-litre car, the old warrior was sadly neglected and could not beat the B.R.M.'s, which were still being highly developed, as was the "Thinwall Special." This one race in 1953 was a rare and exciting affair, recalling the heyday of the 4½-litre Ferrari in 1951, but now it was a swan song that was a pity to see after the stirring fights put up in earlier days. Being badly prepared for this one race the big car split its gearbox after only three laps, and that was the end of the factory 4½-litre cars.

Although the pure Grand Prix car was not due to change until 1954, as laid down in the new Formula 1, the years 1952 and 1953 saw Formula 2 influence many designers, and for those two years we can accept the 2-litre cars as representing full Grand Prix cars. While racing his big 12-cylinder cars Ferrari was also developing the 2-litre version—from which the 4½-litre was evolved—and by the end of 1951 he had realized that the 12-cylinder layout was not the best answer for a small engine and he had built a 2-litre 4-cylinder engine.

This was a very simple unit, with gear-driven overhead camshafts and side-draft Weber carburetors of enormous choke size, there being a pair of double-choke assemblies, giving in effect one carburetor per cylinder. Enzo Ferrari was always very clever in anticipating any probable changes in design envisaged by the F.I.A., and he used this new 4-cylinder car to sway their decision over the matter of the 1954 Formula. It first appeared at the last race of 1951, just as the F.I.A. was making a decision on the engine capacity for the new Formula 1 rules. This first 4-cylinder Ferrari ran in company with the big Ferraris and was of 2½-litres capacity so that the members of the F.I.A. Technical Commission who were present could not help having the idea of an unsupercharged 2½-litre Formula fixed firmly in front of their eyes, and it was no surprise when that decision was made at the end of the 1951 season.

During 1952 this Ferrari design was reduced to 2 litres and had a most successful season, in spite of opposition from many other makes. Formula 2 had been quite active for some time before it became the most important type of racing, and during 1951, when it was playing the part of "voiturette" racing to the really fast cars, the 12-cylinder 2-litre Ferrari had often been seriously challenged by an English team known as H.W.M., the initials of the garage in which they were designed and built.

These cars used 4-cylinder Alta engines, identical to the unit used in the unsuccessful Alta Grand Prix car but now running unsupercharged and with enlarged bore and stroke to give 2 litres capacity. This team was a private venture financed by John Heath and had a chassis designed by him using a number of stock components, such as the front suspension from M.G., steering from Morris Minor and other components from Standard Vanguard, and an Armstong-Siddeley pre-selector gearbox. The rear suspension was a de Dion of Heath's own design and, as a sign of the times, the rear brakes were mounted inboard alongside the differential housing in order to reduce unsprung weight. These successful 4-cylinder Alta-engined cars could often challenge the Ferraris, especially on twisty circuits where the power characteristics of their 4-cyinder engines had a definite advantage over the 12-cylinder units of the Ferraris. It was this fact more than anything else that prompted Ferrari to develop a four-cylinder engine, and during 1952 he realized he had made a very wise move.

1953 Formula II Maserati 6 sylinder 2000cc racing car from which the successful
250F Grand Prix car was developed

7. THE ERA OF THE UNHAPPY B. R. M.

If the 1952 season of 2-litre racing was comparatively slow, it made up for it in variety, for the number of different makes that were competing had never before been so numerous. Maserati returned to racing once more with quite an advanced 6-cylinder 2-litre car, with an entirely new chassis and suspension, while a private team in Italy belonging to Enrico Plate built two cars from old 4CLT Maserati components, using the engine in unsupercharged form and enlarged to 2 litres, in the same way that H.W.M had used the Grand Prix Alta engine.

The Osca firm also made a serious entry into the Formula 2 field with a 6-cylinder car that was new in every respect, and like H.W.M., they too were searching for reduced unsprung weight with a de Dion rear suspension and mounted their brakes "inboard."

Among the other firms to be very active during this new period of racing was Cooper with a very simple chassis and suspension based on their tiny 500 cc racing cars, and using a 2-litre Bristol sports car engine and gearbox. Also from England came the Connaught with a very advanced chassis and suspension, but using a sports Lea-

Connaught Formula II car of 1953 with 4 cylinder 2000cc unsupercharged engine

Francis engine, while both E.R.A. and Frazer-Nash built Formula 2 cars using Bristol engines and gearboxes. The E.R.A. had a very advanced chassis and suspension making great use of light metals, and Frazer-Nash using a single-seater version of their well-proven sports car chassis.

From France came Gordini with his very effective little 6-cylinder 2-litre cars that had been developed from his earlier 1½-litre "voiturette" racing cars. With so many small firms engaged in racing there was never a lack of entries for all the Grand Prix races held during the season, and though engine design lagged badly, there was a great deal of progress made in chassis and suspension design. Many of the constructors, especially in Britain, were tied to using sports car engines due to lack of money or ability to build their own engines, and in consequence they all put their efforts into finding more speed by improving roadholding and braking. Among the many things that were developed during the season were light alloy wheels, improved drum brakes, the development of bi-metal drums, lightweight construction of suspension parts compared with the usual heavy forgings currently in use and other ways of weight saving such as the use of light alloy radiators, and welded fuel tanks instead of the heavier type of riveted tank.

Ferrari and Maserati were content to go on with engine development, relying on sheer horsepower to win their races, but the British teams with their enforced search for speed from the chassis rather than from b.h.p. were setting a basic idea of design that was soon to be followed by everyone. This was the attention to the ratio of the sprung weight to unsprung weight, a vital factor in suspension design. Also they were encouraging the trend to over-all lightweight, a necessity in their designs as their sports-car engines were underpowered compared with the freely-designed Ferrari, Maserati and Osca engines.

In the overall picture of the Grand Prix car the years 1952 and 1953 can really be considered as an interval in general design, during which much detail knowledge was gained to be of use when the new Formula came into being. The development of the unsupercharged engine was now of primary interest, for the 1954 Formula virtually ruled out the use of a supercharged engine and Ferrari and Maserati made great strides with power outputs from their Formula 2 engines.

The 2-Litre Ferrari Type 500

Strictly speaking, the 4-cylinder 2-litre Ferrari does not count as being a Grand Prix car, by our definition, for while it was in use by Scuderia Ferrari in 1952 and 1953 the Grand Prix Formula for the more powerful type of car was still in existence. Because of lack of support, as explained, the Formula 2 cars took pride of place for two years and during this time the 2-litre Ferrari held an almost unbeatable position. And, as the F.I.A. decided that the Drivers Championship for 1952 and 1953 should be decided on Formula 2 events, it was the 4-cylinder Ferrari that enabled Alberto Ascari to be World Champion for those two years.

After developing a 12-cylinder Formula 2 car that was quite successful, Ferrari changed his design tactics. In search of more torque at lower r.p.m. for twisty circuits, he built a 4-cylinder engine. At the same time he used this new engine as some advanced publicity for the 1954 Formula 1, but the original layout was for the 2-litre version and this engine first appeared in a 1951 chassis from the older 12-cylinder 2-litre car.

The first race was at Modena at the end of the 1951 season and two cars were entered, driven by Ascari and Villoresi, and resulted

Alberto Ascari, world champion for 1952 and 1953, driving a Type 500 Ferrari Formula II car in 1953. This is a 2000cc 4 cylinder car

in the former finishing 1st but at the expense of his team mate retiring. After this initial success a team of cars was built for 1952 and in addition a number of similar models were built for sale to private owners. The cars had a wheelbase of 86½ inches and the chassis frame consisted of two large-diameter tubular side-members, with a body frame of small diameter tubing welded to the main chassis and assisting with rigidity. Front suspension was conventional Ferrari, with double wishbones to each wheel and a transverse leaf-spring, while the de Dion rear end was identical to that used on the big Grand Prix cars, using twin radius rods on each side and a sliding vertical guide for the center of the de Dion tube.

The 4-cylinder engine used a bore and stroke of 90 mm x 78 mm giving 1985 cc capacity, and thanks to the very short stroke it ran to 7000 r.p.m. Each cylinder was fed by its own Weber carburetor, these very large single choke instruments being especially designed for this engine. Stub exhaust pipes were used and the engine drove to a 4-speed-and-reverse gearbox that was integral with the rear axle differential housing. On these cars Ferrari dropped the use of a radiator grille, the front of the car having a plain and unadorned opening leading air up a duct to the radiator. The engine was comparatively simple in design and was easy to maintain as well as being very robust. It used two overhead camshafts driven by a train of gears from the front of the engine and two spark plugs to each cylinder, as well as two valves.

During 1952 the factory team competed in 18 races and was only beaten on one occasion. More often than not the team finished in 1-2-3 order, recalling the recent days of the all-conquering Alfa Romeo team. The cars that were sold to private owners also achieved many successes, so that this season of small-time racing was very much a Ferrari benefit. Sometimes Ferrari entered four cars, and the drivers were Ascari, Villoresi, Taruffi and Farina and if only three cars were required then Taruffi was dropped. Although all three drivers who formed the main part of the team were of the highest quality, there was a certain amount of personal rivalry between Ascari and Farina. Quite often the racing scene was enlivened by personal battles between these two with complete disregard for the well-being of the Scuderia Ferrari, but luckily the Type 500 Ferrari was able to stand up to this sort of treatment. At various times during the season one or other of the four works drivers would be replaced for a specific race and the French driver Andre Simon and the Italian drivers Sergio Sighinolfi and Piero Scotti all had drives, while the late Mike Hawthorn had a test-drive at the very end of the season.

Of the production racing cars that were built, the first went to Louis Rosier and the second to the Swiss driver Rudolph Fischer, while later in the season others were built and sold to Robert Baird and the Belgian Ecurie Francorchamps, to be driven by their drivers, Roger Laurent, Charles de Tornaco and Jacques Swaters.

1954 saw the Scuderia Ferrari with a very powerful team of drivers consisting of Ascari, Farina, Villoresi and Hawthorn, and the 4-cylinder cars went from strength to strength. No great changes were made to the design, though improvements were made to such things as carburetor mountings, exhaust systems, brakes and front suspension and one of the greatest assets of the team was the reliability of the cars. Once again Ascari won the World Championship, using the 4-cylinder Ferrari, but towards the end of the season the team received some severe opposition from the Maserati cars and when this phase of unsupercharged Formula 2 racing came to an end the Ferrari was nearly at the end of its development. In two seasons of racing it had achieved a remarkable record and only failed to win on three occasions, once being soundly beaten by Gordini, once being beaten by ill-luck and Maserati, and once through engine failure in the whole team of cars.

With the new Formula approaching, Ferrari tried out his new car in 2-litre form at the end of 1953, this being the Squalo or Type 553, and in 1954 this new car was used alongside the 1952-53 cars which had new engines enlarged to $2\frac{1}{2}$ litres. Of the privately owned 4-cylinder cars Rosier had his fitted with the larger engine, as did the Belgian Equipe; Baird's car was bought by Reg Parnell and similarly brought up to 1954 specification.

During 1953 there were occasional races for cars conforming to the new Formula, in order to give manufacturers a chance of a preview try-out, and both Gordini and Ferrari ran their Formula 2 cars with engines enlarged to $2\frac{1}{2}$ litres, but it was obvious that the new Formula was going to call for completely new designs, not merely adaptations of old designs. It was also clear that when new designs developed, as they certainly would, such small manufacturers as Cooper, H.W.M. and Maserati-Plate who were racing "home-built specials" would certainly have to drop out, for their cars were already out-dated. The Formula 1 was still in force until the end of 1953, even though none of the major Grand Prix events were being held for this category. But on one glorious occasion, in France, a full Formula 1 event was held and a B.R.M. team appeared to challenge a lone works Ferrari $4\frac{1}{2}$-litre and two privately owned ones, and this race was truly the swan song of the large powerful Grand Prix cars of an era that was now dead. After the rather watered-down races that had been happening, this revival of real Grand Prix racing with 400 b.h.p. cars brought the crowd to its feet and both teams blew themselves to pieces so that a privately owned Ferrari won, but it certainly convinced everyone of how exciting the Formula 1 cars had been. If only the B.R.M.

could have put on a similar show at the beginning of the 1952 season, instead of half-way through 1953, then without doubt organizers would have gone on holding Formula 1 races.

The 16-Cylinder Supercharged B.R.M.

The first of these complicated and advanced cars was completed by the end of 1949, though it was not then ready to race, merely being out on test. The 1½-litre engine was a masterpiece of design, having 16 cylinders in two banks of eight, lying in vee formation with 135 degree angle in the vee, the bore and stroke being 49.53 mmx48.26 mm. There were two overhead camshafts to each cylinder bank, and they were driven by a train of gears from the center of the crankshaft. The power take off was also from this point, being by a shaft running parallel with the crankshaft.

A two-stage centrifugal supercharger layout, evolved from knowledge supplied by Rolls Royce Aircraft Division, was mounted on the front of the engine and gave immensely high pressures. But this only worked when the r.p.m. were around 40,000, at which speed the engine was doing 12,000 r.p.m. and giving about 380-400 b.h.p., so that the engine had to run at very high speeds and was thus not an easy one to handle. Mounted in a rather long tubular chassis frame with a 98-inch wheelbase the engine drove to a five-speed gearbox incorporated in the differential assembly. The front suspension was by two trailing arms on each side and at the

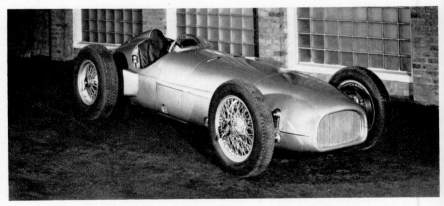

The 16 cylinder B. R. M. racing car of 1949 with supercharged 1500cc engine

rear the layout was de Dion. All four wheels were sprung on tele-scopic compressed air and oil units, developed by Lockheed, while the brakes were special Girling design using three shoes in each drum.

The firm of B.R.M., the initials standing for British Racing Motors, was fathered by Raymond Mays and Peter Berthon and be-tween them they got together numerous interested members of the British motor industry who supplied parts and did specialized work. This perhaps was the real reason for the slow progress of the B.R.M., for too much time was spent running around after firms that were giving "free gifts" in their own time, with little apprecia-tion of the urgency that is required by Grand Prix racing. In May 1950 the first car gave a demonstration at Silverstone, which was very fine except that by this time it should have been competing.

At the B.D.R.C. meeting at Silverstone in August of that year two cars were entered, with four drivers nominated, so typical of the muddled thinking that was going on behind the project. These were Raymond Mays and Parnell on the first car and Raymond Sommer and Peter Walker on the second. As it happened only one car was ready to race, and that at the last moment, so it was given to Ray-mond Sommer, he being the most experienced Grand Prix driver of the four. This first race appearance was a complete fiasco, for a drive shaft broke as he let in the clutch at the start and the car rolled to an inglorious stop after travelling only a few yards.

Towards the end of the season Parnell drove the car in two small meetings at Goodwood, and prospects looked better, for though there was little opposition, he did at least win both events. Encouraged by this, two cars were taken to Spain for the Grand Prix at Barcelona at the end of the season, and were driven by Parnell and Walker. Although both cars had to retire, they put up a reasonable showing while they ran and gave promise of better things in 1951.

As it turned out, the 1951 season was disastrous for the B.R.M. team. They went from one withdrawal to the next, entering for five events and four times failing to appear on the starting grid. The only time they raced was in the British Grand Prix at Silver-stone, where they started without having practiced, and though both cars finished the race, both Parnell and Peter Walker suffered severe burns from the overheated cockpits and they were never in the running, this race being the classic Ferrari versus Alfa Romeo "needle match." It had seemed reasonable to suppose that the B.R.M. cars would join in the battle with the two Italian teams during 1951, but they went from one unfortunate episode to the next, the cars seldom being ready in time. Even when they were ready last minute troubles arose, and it finally became obvious that big time Grand Prix racing was a bit beyond the capabilities of the people behind the B.R.M. team. The cars remained virtually unchanged throughout the season, all the efforts of the factory being needed to get them in a raceworthy condition without having time left over for development.

The whole conception of the car was so complicated that even the smallest job of work took longer than was justified, and getting most of the parts made outside of the Bourne factory meant innumerable delays and quite often inferior workmanship that was not discovered until very late in the assembly. The 16-cylinder supercharged engine was not a unit to be hurriedly assembled overnight, nor was it a simple one to change, so that the slightest engine trouble meant many hours of hard work by mechanics who had little previous knowledge of working on such complicated machinery. No doubt, had the Alfa Romeo factory been given the car they would have developed it very rapidly into a world beater, for it certainly had every possibility and Alfa Romeo with their vast resources and knowledge could have dealt with the project. The B.R.M. organization was quite simply too small for such an enormous undertaking, and by the end of the 1951 season nobody was taking the cars very seriously anymore.

At the beginning of the 1952 season the team did a strange thing that was to influence the whole future of Grand Prix racing. Alfa Romeo, Talbot and Simca had all announced their withdrawal from Formula 1 Grand Prix racing, leaving only Ferrari and a few private owners, so that attention was turning towards Formula 2 cars. While the B.R.M. team was at Italy's Monza Autodrome doing extensive testing, the Italians put on a Grand Prix at Turin, expecting B.R.M. to enter and compete against the Ferrari team.

Although they were only a few miles away the Bourne team ignored the Turin race, saying they were too busy doing test work, and it was this fiasco of a race at Turin, which was a Ferrari benefit, that decided organizers all over Europe to drop Formula 1 in favor of the smaller 2-litre unsupercharged cars. It is certain that had B.R.M. entered their team for the Turin race—no matter how they finished—race organizers would have kept Formula 1 alive during 1952.

As it was there was only one event, at Albi in France, together with some small British events. Once they got started in 1952 the B.R.M. made good progress, not only starting in those events that were available but going extremely fast while they were running. However, reliability still escaped them and the cars were beset by one trouble after another but at least they were gaining racing experience and the cars could now be taken seriously. But it was two years too late.

Among the drivers who tried their hand at racing these frustrating cars during 1952 were Fangio, Gonzalez, Stirling Moss, Parnell, and Ken Wharton, but none of them were completely happy in the team. If they were not upset by having to race without practice because their cars weren't ready in time, they were annoyed by minor breakdowns or basic faults that should have been eradicated on the test bed. If these weren't enough then they found difficulty in controlling the car, especially in the rain, for although the engine was now giving immense power—about 400 b.h.p.—it was at engine speeds in the region of 10,000-12,000 r.p.m. and anywhere below that the power dropped off suddenly, making the car rather vicious. During the season modifications were made, in particular to the cooling of the water and oil, and new Girling disc brakes were fitted, this being their first experiments in this type of braking system.

By the end of 1952 the cars were in a reasonable raceworthy condition, and at a small race at Goodwood they rounded off their activities by finishing 1-2-3. But the whole project had gotten so out of hand that Mays and Berthon realized they would have to stop before they went broke, so the whole of the B.R.M. project was put up for sale. It was bought by Mr. Alfred Owen, the head of a large group of engineering firms known as the Owen Group, and he agreed to keep the project going as a private venture. This he did, and though Formula 1 was virtually dead in Europe in 1953 the B.R.M. went on through a large development program and raced continually in small British National events run to a Formula Libre category.

With Parnell and Wharton driving in the beginning of the season the cars had numerous successes, but as the opposition was negligible its activities were never taken very seriously. Later, when Fangio and Gonzalez drove the cars, the victories were very hollow and counted for nothing, for by now most people were eyeing the new Formula 1 due to begin in 1954, and Ferrari and Gordini were already racing prototypes for this 2½-litre limit. In Europe the only Formula 1 event in 1953 was at Albi. Three B.R.M.s were driven by Fangio, Gonzalez and Wharton, and though they had complete command of the race they failed to win because of constant tire troubles on this very high speed road circuit. But it was notable that they were reaching speeds in the region of 180 m.p.h., and Fangio set up a lap record at 115.57 m.p.h.

The 16-cylinder engines were now standing up to more than 60 lbs/sq. in. of supercharger pressure and developing nearly 450 b.h.p. so that without doubt they were the most powerful cars designed to the 1947-53 Formula for Grand Prix cars. But they had arrived too late, and had achieved these remarkable figures after everyone else had packed up and gone home. With the new Formula taking over in 1954 and most people ready for it, B.R.M. were still working on the design of their new car.

They continued to race the supercharged 1½-litres, but now there were only English Club events available for them. Of the three cars that had been built, one was completely demolished in a crash in 1953 but the other two were still kept raceworthy. However, as the only available races were very short ones, they built two new cars—known as Mark II models—which were six inches shorter in the wheelbase, and very much lighter. They were in effect sprint versions of the original cars and during the season these two new cars were raced and occasionally they were supported by one of the old cars, but the whole affair had now become very much a British national affair, and International motor racing circles no longer paid much attention to the B.R.M.

Before the season began Wharton was sent to New Zealand with one of the old cars, but the appearances were not very successful, the car proving unreliable, though it did give people outside of Europe a chance to hear the incredible exhaust note of the wonderful engine. The Mark II models had new chassis frames, built of two large-diameter tubes, the same engine, gearbox, and front suspension as the Mark I. However, the de Dion rear end was altered, now having the accepted arrangement for Grand Prix cars of two radius rods running forwards from each end of the de Dion tube, with the tube being in one piece. Previously the engine had used coil ignition, but it was now changed to magnetic ignition, while short stub exhaust pipes were fitted. The noise from these stubs was truly incredible, so much so that some English circuits would not tolerate the noise and demanded that long tail pipes should be fitted. They were still persevering with disc brakes, and though they were proving very powerful they were not devoid of trouble and the Mark II cars became noted for their habits of spinning. In this short chassis form they were exceedingly fierce motor cars, and the slightest mistake by the driver would provoke fantastic wheelspin and put the car sideways, so that the slightest malfunctioning of a brake was impossible to control.

Ken Wharton and Ron Flockhart were the drivers during this last season of the supercharged B.R.M. and they had numerous successes. At the end of the 1954 season the two cars raced at Aintree in a Formula Libre event, and it was interesting that the best that Flockhart could do was to finish 3rd behind two of the new 250F Maseratis, thus demonstrating that the new Grand Prix Formula cars were rapidly replacing the era of supercharging and thus justifying the new Formula.

This was the last appearance of the supercharged 16-cylinder B.R.M. cars and after that down to serious work on the cars for the new Formula. While the Alfa Romeo 158 and 159 represented the pinnacle of engine development to the 1947-53 Formula, the 16-cylinder B.R.M. engine was the pinnacle of engine design of that interesting but vanished era of Grand Prix racing.

Sergio Mantovani driving a 1954 250F 2500cc Grand Prix Maserati

8. 1954: HOW THEY TACKLED THE NEW FORMULA

With the beginning of the 1954 season the new Formula came
into force, with its simple rules that asked for supercharged cars
to have an engine limit of 750cc and unsupercharged cars to have
a limit of 2500cc, while organizers were asked to ensure that races
lasted a minium of three hours or be at least 300 miles in length.
Ferrari and Gordini were naturally well in front, having raced
prototypes during 1953, though of the two the Italian firm was in
the better position. Not only had Ferrari raced his 1952-53 Formula
2 car with engine enlarged to 2½ litres, this being the Type 625,
but he had also tried out a brand new car at the end of the 1953
season.

This car was an entirely new departure in chassis design for
Ferrari, for it used a "space frame" chassis. This is a rectangular
box-like frame constructed of small diameter tubing forming a lat-
tice work, in place of the "ladder-type" frame which has two large
diameter tubes forming chassis side-members and being stressed as
a simple beam in bending. This principle of "space-frame" was not
new by any means, having been used by Cisitalia in their revolutionary but still-born 12-cylinder car of 1949, and also by a number
of British sports car special builders, such as Cooper and Buckler.

The new Ferrari for 1954 was known as the Type 553 and nick-
named "The Squalo," this being the Italian for whale. The general

aspect of the car **was** that of a whale, as it carried the fuel in tanks disposed on each side of the cockpit and thus had a somewhat bloated and bulbous look.

The general suspension principles were as used on the Type 625 car, though the rear axle/gearbox unit was re-designed and had the de Dion tube crossing the car in front of the final drive instead of behind as before. This allowed easy access to a train of transfer gears in the back of the axle unit which could be changed quickly to effect a difference in overall gear ratio for any given circuit. It also fitted in with the general design layout of the whole car, which was to concentrate as much weight as possible within the wheelbase.

Having raced both these cars during 1953, Ferrari was in a happy position when the new season started and seemed confident of success, but his regular rival from Modena, the Maserati team, was also in the field with a brand new car. This had much in common with the Squalo Ferrari, having a space frame, and the de Dion tube mounted forward of the transmission instead of behind it as most people had been doing. The engine was a six-cylinder based on the knowledge gained from the 1952-53 Formula 2 car, but it was greatly redesigned in detail. A completely new gearbox/differential unit was made, this being in one and mounted on the rear of the chassis, with the gearbox shafts running across the car and driving to the final-drive pinion by spur gears, the change of direction from the propshaft to the half-shafts being effected by bevels on the input side of the gearbox. Front suspension was a development of the Formula 2 car, being of double wishbones and coil springs, while a transverse leaf spring controlled the de Dion layout at the rear, as on the Ferrari.

Unlike the Maranello design there was no attempt to concentrate weight within the wheelbase, the Maserati having a large fuel tank which formed the tail and also an oil tank in the tail. This new Maserati, known as the Type 250F, was to prove one of the most successful designs of the new Formula and, unlike Ferrari, the Maserati concern made their new model for sale to race-drivers, as well as running a factory team.

By a happy combination of weight distribution and steering characteristics the 250F proved to be a very raceworthy car and one that was extremely well mannered, suited to almost any circuit and easy to drive. The "Squalo" Ferrari, however, was exactly the opposite and was never successful because its handling characteristics demanded new techniques which the Ferrari team drivers seemed reluctant to learn. The older Ferrari design, the Type 625, although having some success was soon outdated by newer designs.

The season opened with Maserati in a strong position with their new car, and Ferrari having a busy time trying to sort out his new one, develop the old one and not being sure just which road to follow, while Gordini was racing his enlarged Formula 2 car that obviously could not keep up for long with the new ideas of racing car construction. In the same way H.W.M. were soon left behind, having only their old Formula 2 car to race with an enlarged engine, being financially incapable of building new designs. Cooper also dropped from the scene for want of a suitable power unit, having to rely on engine manufacturers as their own resources only ran to chassis building. But Connaught on the other hand were going ahead with a completely new car using a new Alta engine, though still a 4-cylinder.

While the early part of the season was sorting out those who were going ahead in the new Formula 1 Grand Prix events and those who were returning to sports car racing, such as Osca and Cooper, or those who were giving up altogether, there were rumors that the two great automobile factories of Lancia and Daimler-Benz were well ahead with the building of cars for the new Formula. It was not long before these rumors proved to be true, as prototypes were seen out on test, and it soon became common knowledge that both firms had built brand new cars, both revolutionary in their own way, and that Grand Prix racing was returning from the playground of the amateur and small concerns to the serious test-bed for the big firms in the automobile industry.

The name of Daimler-Benz needed no introduction, their highly developed Mercedes-Benz cars of the 1934-39 period being still fresh in many memories, though the name of Lancia had never before been connected with modern Grand Prix racing. However, some idea of what might be expected could be gained from the highly efficient team of sports cars raced by the Turin firm during the previous two years, their performance in winning the Mille Miglia and the Mexican Road Race still being in the news.

Bearing in mind that the new Maserati owed a lot of its ancestry to knowledge gained in Formula 2, as did the Squalo Ferrari, especially as regards the engine and suspension, the designs of the Mercedes-Benz and the Lancia could be viewed as starting from scratch and building especially for the 1954 Formula. It is interesting to compare these two in detail, for though they were both unsupercharged 8-cylinder 2½-litre cars, the resemblance ended there. That two teams of designers could produce such widely differing designs for the same Formula was one of the highlights of 1954.

The New Mercedes

The Mercedes-Benz designated the Type W196 and Dr. Nallinger and his team of designers, headed by Rudolph Uhlenhaut, used a straight-eight cylinder layout for the engine. It employed two overhead camshafts, these being driven from the center of the crankshaft by a train of spur gears, while the power take-off was also from the center gear on the crankshaft, with a shaft running rearwards to the clutch, this principle having been used by B.R.M.

The fully streamlined W196 Mercedes-Benz Formula I Grand Prix car of 1954

on their old supercharged 16-cylinder car. The Mercedes-Benz engine designers perfected an old idea for their new engine, in having the inlet and exhaust valves opened *and* closed by cams and rockers, there being no valve springs and in consequence no limit on the r.p.m. This method of fully mechanical valve operation was known as "desmodromic" and had been experimented with by various engineers many years before but dropped because of unreliability and complication.

The Daimler-Benz engineers perfected this idea and with it they designed a system, in conjunction with the firm of Robert Bosch, of direct and controlled fuel-injection into the cylinders. This did away at one fell swoop with the two difficulties attached to the extraction of power from an internal combustion engine—complete control of valve timing and fuel/air mixture. The previous problems had stemmed from the fact that spring-returned valves are always subject to the whims of the characteristics of springs, and carburetors are far from perfect, invariably supplying the correct fuel/air mixture only at various parts of the power curve, never the whole way through it.

This straight-eight engine was of necessity a rather large unit and in order to fit into the general layout of the complete car it was laid on its side, a few degrees from the horizontal, and the power shaft ran to the rear of the car where a 5-speed, all-syncromesh gearbox was built in unit with the final drive assembly. The mechanical components were surrounded by a perfect "space-frame" constructed of very small diameter steel tubing, and suspension was independent to all four wheels. At the front double wishbones and torsion bars were used, while at the rear a swing-axle layout was employed, also with torsion bars, this rear suspension breaking new ground in swing-axle design by having the pivoting center mounted below the center of the differential unit, thus giving a low rear roll center.

Remarkably large drum brakes were used, one on each wheel. All four were mounted "inboard," the two front ones side by side behind the radiator, the rear ones on each side of the differential unit. In the original specification for this revolutionary design, provision was made for optional four-wheel drive on similar lines to that of the 12-cylinder Cisitalia. The drive to the front wheels of the Mercedes-Benz was to be operational by a foot switch, rather like a dipper-switch. It was for this reason that the design included such complexities as inboard brakes, with the need for drive shafts and universal swivels for the steering pins. This also resulted in the gearbox part of the final drive layout being set to the left to allow a forward running power shaft for the front wheels, and the engine being placed on its side to permit space underneath it for the drive shaft.

As it turned out, time was too short to complete design of the four-wheel drive project, and when the Stuttgart engineers found that the car was powerful enough to deal with all opposition in rear wheel drive form, the original scheme was dropped. As can be imagined, this complicated piece of machinery was large and rather heavy, but this did not worry Daimler-Benz. They covered the whole thing with a fully streamlined bodywork, being sublimely confident that their very advanced engine would develop close to 300 b.h.p., (which it ultimately did) which would be far more than any other Grand Prix car.

Enter The Lancia D50

While development and testing of this German car was progressing, the Lancia D50 was also nearing completion. The Turin engineers, led by Vittorio Jano, who had been with Alfa Romeo for many years and had inspired the Type 158 car way back in 1938 which he let Colombo develop, had tackled the new Formula in a completely different manner. They had designed a fairly straightforward 8-cylinder of vee formation using a wide angle of 90 degrees, with overhead camshafts driven by duplex chains and four double-choke carburetors mounted in the vee. This power unit was not expected to deliver much more than 250-260 b.h.p., so the rest of the car was built with one thing in mind—low weight and compactness. This they achieved, using a very light space-frame in which the engine itself formed part of the structure, the front suspension being bolted to the cylinder heads at the front of the

The 1955 Lancia D50 driven by Alberto Ascari in the Monaco Grand Prix

camboxes, and the center section of the frame, forming the bulkhead and cockpit, being bolted to the rear of the cylinder heads.

Throughout the car everything was pared down to the very minimum in size and weight, and, like Ferrari, Jano concentrated on getting all the weight within the wheelbase. To this end he carried his fuel in pannier tanks mounted on struts sticking out from the body and lying between the front and rear wheels on each side. In order to keep the center of gravity low, the driver sat well down in the car and the propellor shaft ran alongside his seat, this being brought about by mounting the engine at an angle in the chassis. The gearbox followed typical Italian practice, being in unit with the differential and final drive gears, and, like Maserati, the Lancia turned its drive by bevels to a transverse line before it entered the gearbox, the drive from the output of the gearbox going to the wheels through a series of spur gears. The Lancia was as small and compact as the Mercedes-Benz was large and ungainly, yet they both represented new and advanced ideas of Grand Prix cars, were both of equal technical merit, and on the one occasion they raced against each other in 1954 they proved of virtually equal performance.

9. THE SHORT HAPPY LIFE OF THE LANCIA

While the 1954 season began with Maserati in the ascendant—
Ferrari still being rather confused by his variety of designs—Mercedes-Benz came along at mid-season and swept away all opposition
at their first outing, on a circuit particularly well suited to their
streamlined cars. The race following this they suffered a severe set-
back when they discovered that on a twisty circuit the fully-
streamlined body hampered visibility, and Ferrari was thus able to
take the lead.

However, it did not take Mercedes-Benz long to redesign the
bodywork, using a type on which the four road wheels were fully
exposed, and though the car looked rather ungainly it was effective
enough to win the next two races. Lancia were rather a long time in
joining in the actual racing as their cars called for a new driving
technique, somewhat like the Squalo Ferrari. Rather than race before their drivers were fully accustomed to the car, they held back
until sufficient practice had been completed, and this was not until
the last race of the season. On this epic occasion, at Barcelona for
the Spanish Grand Prix, the front row of the start of the race saw
four entirely different designs of Grand Prix car—Lancia, Mercedes-Benz, Maserati and Ferrari. They appeared to have speed and
performance in that exact order, although the race was won by
Ferrari with a modified Squalo car due to unreliability and mechanical misfortunes in the newer designs.

The D50 Lancia Grand Prix Car

The life of the Lancia Grand Prix car was exceedingly short
and quite sweet, for it first appeared at the Spanish Grand Prix in
October 1954 and the whole project had been abandoned by July

1955. It had been planned as an entirely new conception of Grand Prix car with remarkable attention being paid to lightness, though in consequence there was little margin left for development. After a rather long testing period that took place throughout most of the 1954 season, two cars, to be driven by Ascari and Villoresi, were entered for the last race of that year. The whole set-up of the Scuderia Lancia was one of unlimited money and effort, almost on a scale equal to that of the Mercedes-Benz team, and on this first outing the cars showed a promise justifying the obvious initial expense of producing them.

In face of the strongest opposition seen at a Grand Prix race for many years, the two Lancias made 1st and 2nd fastest practice qualifying times on the first appearance, and even at the end of the second day's practice no one had beaten Ascari's lap time. In the intial rush of the race Ascari was up with the leaders, and after three laps he got in front and then drew away at the rate of 2 seconds per lap. Unfortunately, however, after only 10 laps the car was withdrawn with reported clutch trouble, and Villoresi had already dropped out for the same reason.

After waiting all season for the appearance of these unusual cars from Turin their performance was regrettably short, but they were certainly impressive while they lasted. They next appeared in the beginning of 1955 in the Argentine Grand Prix, three of them being driven by Ascari, Villoresi and Castelotti. While they showed good speed on the twisty Buenos Aires circuit, they did not seem to have very good handling qualities and all three cars retired due to spinning off the course, luckily without any damage to the drivers.

Before the next big Grand Prix event they ran in three small races, on each occasion being opposed by only Maserati or Ferrari. In the first race, at Turin, they finished 1-3-4, in the order Ascari, Villoresi, Castellotti, and then they went to Pau, in southwest France, where certain victory was snatched from Ascari only a few laps before the finish due to a brake pipe splitting. This resulted in Ascari finishing 2nd, Villoresi 4th and Castellotti 5th. The third of these small races was at Naples and here only Ascari and Villoresi took part, the former winning and the latter finishing 3rd.

After this interlude, during which time the team had gained valuable racing experience, they went to the Monaco Grand Prix, where all the big teams competed. Four cars were entered, with Louis Chiron added to the three regular drivers, and there was a fifth car at the circuit as a spare, which indicated to what extent the Lancia organization was going in for racing. It was Ascari who kept up with the all-conquering Mercedes-Benz cars, and he might well have achieved victory when the German cars failed had he not skidded off the course and crashed into the harbor. Castellotti began by backing up his team leader but then bent a wheel on a curb and the resultant stop at the pits to have it changed dropped him a long way back.

He had to drive brilliantly to come in second. Villoresi was never in the running, finishing 5th, and Chiron found the car quite beyond his ability, finishing a distant 6th.

There was no doubt that the Lancia team was a severe threat to the German cars, but shortly after the Monte Carlo race they went completely to pieces. First of all Ascari was killed in a sports car crash, and this not only caused his very good friend Villoresi to temporarily lose interest in racing, but so depressed the entire Lancia racing organization that they virtually withdrew from compeition. A lone entry was made for the Belgian Grand Prix with Castellotti as driver, and he beat the entire Mercedes-Benz team, as well as Ferrari and Maserati, in practice, but in the race was lying third behind Fangio and Moss when a seized gearbox put him out of the race. At the same time Lancia was having financial difficulties in Italy, and after some weeks of tension the whole affair was settled by the Lancià family selling their interest in the firm, and their whole racing program was abandoned overnight.

Later it was decided that all the cars, spares, design and equipment would be given to the Scuderia Ferrari as a gift to encourage him to continue the struggles on behalf of Italy in Grand Prix racing, and this was carried out by the end of the summer of 1955. The cars appeared again that season under the banner of the Scuderia Ferrari, for the Italian Grand Prix at Monza, but after running into tire troubles in practice they were withdrawn before the race began. They would have been driven by Farina, who was signed up with Ferrari, and Villoresi and Castellotti who had been taken on with the gift of the cars and equipment.

Following this unfortunate appearance, two cars were sent to England for the Gold Cup race at Oulton Park, with Castellotti and Mike Hawthorn as drivers. The opposition was not up to World Championship standards, and Hawthorn made the fastest practice lap and finished second in the race, while Castellotti, who was not very satisfied with the road holding of his car, finished a long way back. This was the last appearance of the Lancia Grand Prix cars as orginally designed, for the following year Ferrari made drastic alterations to them and they became Lancia/Ferraris.

In the form as laid down by Vittorio Jano, their designer, and as built in the Turin factory of the Lancia Motor Company, the cars were raced for almost exactly one year—from October 1954 to October 1955—during which time they showed every prospect of being capable of challenging the best in Grand Prix racing. But, due to a series of misfortunes within the firm, all they added up to was a very expensive and glorious "final fling" on the part of young Gianni Lancia, the son of the famous founder of the firm. It is interesting that the head of the Lancia family had supported racing in the early days of automobile racing and then withdrawn to concentrate of building production cars and never again built a racing Lancia. The D50 was built by his son after the founder of the firm had died, and within a very short time financial ruin overtook the business, just as had been predicted by him when giving his reasons for not supporting racing. Of course, it is quite possible that financial ruin was on the way inevitably, and that Gianni Lancia simply decided to have this last glorious and expensive go at racing before the firm had to be sold.

The First Vanwall

All this building and racing was more than justifying the new Formula, and there was a feeling that Grand Prix racing had returned to its true status after the doldrums of 1952 and 1953. The only disappointment was that Alfa Romeo was no longer interested in racing, being fully occupied with new production projects. France had dropped right out of the running, though Gordini was still racing his out-dated cars and was working slowly on a new eight-cylinder design, but he lacked the finance and resources of his rivals. In England there was much interest in this new Formula and B.R.M. was completing the design of a new car, having at last abandoned the supercharged 16-cylinder job which they had been racing in National events.

Their keen rivals, the Vandervell stable, now produced a proto-type for the new Formula, running it a few events in 1954. This was a compartively simple 4-cylinder car with an engine built from knowledge gleaned from Norton racing motorcycles, Mr. Vander-vell having previously been a director of Norton Motors. Suspen-sion was based on the 4½-litre Ferrari, as was the gearbox and final drive, while Cooper built a simple "space-frame" to Vander-vell's specification. One outstanding feature of this car that was to have far-reaching effects was the brakes. These were of the disc or spot type, built by Vandervell to patents loaned by the Goodyear Company, and had been perfected on his old 4½-litre "Thinwall Special" during its seasons of British National racing. This new car from the Vandervell factory, a precision concern manufac-turing shell bearings under the name of Thinwall Bearings, was called the "Vanwall Special."

Another project that was completed before the end of the sea-son, but which did not race until 1955, was the Connaught. This small concern was rather like Gordini, in that money was limited though bright ideas were not, and progress in building was slow. The Connaught used a simple ladder-type chassis with suspension derived from their Formula 2 car of 1953 and had a much modified 2½-litre 4-cylinder Alta engine coupled to a pre-selector gearbox. Like Mercedes-Benz, the Connaught designers went forward with a fully-streamlined bodywork covering the wheels, and like Van-dervell they employed disc brakes, these being of Girling design. The object behind these plans was similar to Maserati, in that the cars were to be offered for sale as well as being raced by the factory themselves.

1954 Connaught 4 cylinder 2500cc Grand Prix car with full aero-dynamic bodywork

10. MERCEDES TAKES OVER

The 1955 season was a tumultuous one in many ways, for it started with a battle between the four leading makes in the Argentine series of races, which Mercedes-Benz won after a hard fight. And then when the scene turned to Europe, the powerful German firm suffered ignoble defeat when all their cars broke down in the Monte Carlo race. Lancia, Maserati and the new Ferrari also had troubles and it was left to the old Type 625 Ferrari to win. However, as the season progressed the Mercedes-Benz team forcibly swept all before them, going from victory to victory and dominating the scene so thoroughly that the Italians were virtually racing among themselves at the back of the field.

Very occasionally the Maserati put up a small challenge to the silver cars from Stuttgart, but they never succeeded in beating them, while Ferrari sunk lower and lower and almost disappeared

Unusual view of the 1955 W196 Mercedes-Benz with the exposed wheel type of bodywork

from the picture. He was still undecided about which of his two 4-cylinder cars to develop, for while the Type 625 was not fast or powerful enough to put up a challenge, the drivers found it both reliable and easy to drive. On the other hand the new Type 555 or Super Squalo, a development of the original car, had more promise but the drivers did not like its handling characteristics.

During the season the new cars from England began to make progress, the Connaught appearing a number of times, as did the Vanwall, while at the end of the season the B.R.M. made its first appearance. In France Gordini was still struggling along, and he built an entirely new car that was interesting technically but too heavy and too underpowered to be a serious rival to the Germans or the Italians. This car had a straight-eight cylinder engine, with two overhead camshafts, and the chassis had independent suspension to all four wheels. The bodywork was a compromise between the all-enveloping type and the normal single-seater Grand Prix type, the object being to improve the aerodynamics of the car.

This question of streamlined bodywork was still very much in the minds of designers, and though Mercedes-Benz had dropped it for most circuits, they still had it for fast circuits such as Monza. The new Connaught also had a fully enveloping bodywork, but they too reverted to the normal single-seater layout with exposed wheels, one of their main objections to the streamlined bodywork being the vulnerability in a slight excursion off the road and the enormous expense of repairs. As far as an increase of speed was concerned they were convinced of its advantage, while due to having a fairly forward driving position they were not troubled by poor visibility. Mercedes-Benz, on the other hand, had a very rearward seating and on anything other than a high-speed circuit the inability to see the front wheels proved a handicap to the drivers. The whole question of aero-dynamics in relations to the Grand Prix car was being studied by a great many people and there was little doubt that it was going to play a vital part in future designs.

At the end of the season the three British contenders, Connaught, B.R.M. and Vanwall, were beginning to show positive promise. Connaught had a convincing victory in one of the smaller Italian races, admittedly without any opposition from Mercedes-Benz or Ferrari, while the other two makes were beginning to put up good performances in National races. All three were very serious contenders from the point of view of originality and design, the Vanwall putting great store by engine power and braking, the B.R.M. relying on overall smallness and light weight, with less power, and Connaught concentrating on road holding and cornering power.

All three cars were using disc brakes, two having British components. Gordini was also working on disc brakes in conjunction with the French Messier firm, through the Italians and Germans were still relying on drum brakes. While the Italian brake design was fairly orthodox, the Germans had developed drum brakes to a high degree, having both shoes moving outwards instead of being pivoted at one end, and having automatic adjustment to compensate for wear, while being mounted inboard they could be of enormous diameter and width.

While the Italians were struggling to attain the standard set by the Mercedes-Benz team, and the English were just beginning to get their cars raceworthy, the Germans were forging ahead with a program of development that was breathtaking. During the season they modified the design of the W196 car so that they had a variation to suit any circuit. They built cars with three wheelbase lengths; the original long chassis job, a very short one for twisty circuits such as Monte Carlo, and a medium length model.

They had two types of bodywork—fully streamlined or with the wheels exposed—and they had front braking systems with inboard mounted brakes and with hub-mounted brakes. They developed adjustable shock absorbers for the rear so that the driver could alter the setting as his fuel load diminished, and they were continually increasing the power output from the eight-cylinder, fuel-injected engine, and the desmodromic valve gear layout was made throughly reliable. Although they did not achieve 100% reliability throughout the whole car, they did manage a classic finish on one occasion, entering four cars and finishing 1-2-3-4. Throughout 1955 they won every race in which they finished, failing to win one lone event due to all three cars retiring, but they had the satisfaction of being 1st and 2nd at the time of their breakdown.

To the racing world in general they produced a bombshell at the end of the season by announcing their complete withdrawal from all racing activity, just as Alfa Romeo had done in 1949. To the other contenders for Grand Prix honors this was a great relief, but to the racing world it was a considerable loss, for the technical developments of Daimler-Benz were greatly missed. Earlier in the season another bombshell had arrive from Turin when the great Lancia factory went bankrupt and was bought up by Fiat, and the D50 Lancia Grand Prix team was disbanded just as it was beginning to provide serious opposition to Mercedes-Benz. However, the Italian picture brightened up when, as previously mentioned, the entire Lancia operation was handed over to the Scuderia Ferrari.

Having set a furious pace throughout 1955, both from the racing point of view and technically, the withdrawal of Daimler-Benz left the mechanical side of Grand Prix racing rather flat in comparison. But at least everyone else was on a comparatively equal footing, especially as regards finances and facilities, for the scale with which the great Daimler-Benz concern had tackled their racing was breathtaking, compared even with Ferrari or Maserati.

The Mercedes-Benz W196

When Daimler-Benz announced that they were going back into Grand Prix racing in 1954 with the new Formula 1 it aroused great interest, for they had always tackled the problem of motor racing with unlimited resources, and had consistently produced revolutionary motorcars. The first appearance of the 1954 Grand Prix Mercedes-Benz was at the French Grand Prix in July, held that year at Reims, and the expected technical masterpiece from Stuttgart gave no disappointment to anyone. After extensive testing, the cars came to the line perfectly prepared for their first race—with Fangio, Karl Kling and Hans Herrmann as the team drivers—and the first two simply ran away with the race, finishing 1st and 2nd without even being pressed. Herrmann suffered from an engine breakdown but nevertheless recorded the fastest lap, so that re-entry of the Mercedes-Benz team into Grand Prix racing was an unqualified triumph.

This success was short-lived, however, for the next race was at Silverstone in England, with only Fangio and Kling as drivers, and on the rather badly defined aerodrome circuit the streamlined bodies of the Mercedes-Benz hampered vision and the best they could do was fourth place for Fangio and a 7th for Kling, while the team-leader's car also suffered from gearbox trouble.

Before the next big race of 1954, which was the German Grand Prix on the infamous Nurburgring, the cars were fitted with new bodywork which exposed the four wheels, thus making driver visibility much better, and Fangio, Kling and Herman Lang had these redesigned cars while Hans Herrmann had one of the fully stream-lined models. Fangio dominated the race after a brief scuffle at the beginning with the best of the Ferraris, and the German populace

1954 Mercedes-Benz W196 Formula I Grand Prix car 2500cc 8 cylinder with open wheel type bodywork

was overjoyed to see the Mercedes-Benz win their own national Grand Prix.

At one time in the race Lang was running 2nd and Kling 3rd, so that Mercedes-Benz cars lay 1-2-3 in complete domination of the Grand Prix scene, a grim foretaste of what was to come. On this occasion, however, in their third race, the situation did not last. Lang's engine seized and caused him to spin off the road and Kling was delayed by a broken torsion bar mounting on the rear suspension. Fangio went on his unassailable way to finish 1st, while Kling struggled home in 4th place and Herrmann retired with a fuel leak. In the Swiss Grand Prix at Berne, on the now defunct Bremgarten circuit, Fangio once more dominated the race, leading from start to finish, but his team mates Kling and Herrmann were not so lucky. On the opening lap Kling spun round on a hairpin and stalled his motor, but managed to re-start on his own and then drove splendidly to regain ground and get into third place. It was all to no avail, though, for his fuel feed to the injection pump failed and he was forced to retire anyway. The third man of the team, Herrmann, drove a steady but not very fast race, and by reason of other cars retiring he managed to finish 3rd.

For the Italian Grand Prix at Monza, Fangio and Kling used the original cars with fully streamlined bodywork, while Herrmann had one of the exposed wheel cars. It was expected that the streamlined cars would leave all the opposition behind on the fast Monza road circuit, but both Ferrari and Maserati managed to provide some serious opposition for a time. Eventually Fangio triumphed once again due to sheer reliability and stamina, though the other two cars were less fortunate. Kling suffered from an oil leak which sprayed onto his goggles and he missed a turn and went off the road, bending the car but escaping personal injury, while Herrmann had a long pit stop to have all the 16 spark plugs changed and could do no better than a remote 4th.

After this three streamlined cars were taken to the Avus track near Berlin, more as a demonstration of Mercedes-Benz capabilities than a serious motor race, for there was no opposition to the silver cars. The three team drivers drove in close formation throughout the race on this very fast circuit, with Kling, Fangio and Herrmann finishing in that order the winner averaging 132.6 m.p.h. Fangio made the fastest lap at a speed of 139.1 m.p.h.

To close the 1954 season the team went to Barcelona for the Spanish Grand Prix, taking with them some fully streamlined cars and some of the exposed-wheel cars. After practice they decided to use the un-streamlined versions. This ability to take extra cars to a race was typical of the force behind the Mercedes-Benz team, and though they did not achieve complete domination of the scene in their first season, they were wearing down the opposition by sheer weight of material. On sheer speed the cars were not now ahead of their rivals, for the Italian teams had been spurred on to greater efforts by the pace set by the Germans, and the new Lancia team was then showing great promise.

The German cars had 20 or 30 more horsepower than their rivals, but they also weighed a great deal more—the streamlined car being as much as 200 pounds heavier than the Italian cars—and by the end of the season there was little to choose between the performance of the Mercedes-Benz and the three Italian makes— Ferrari, Maserati and Lancia—though the Germans obviously had a better future as far as development of the existing design was concerned.

In the Spanish race Fangio was the fastest of the silver cars but he could not get into the lead, and the best he achieved was 2nd place for a brief time, due to other cars breaking down; then he suffered a bad oil leak and had to slow down, eventually finishing 3rd. Kling was never in the running at all, while Herrmann had to retire with a slipping clutch.

Although Fangio won the World Championship in 1954, and Mercedes-Benz were the victorious manufacturers for the season, the domination they showed on their first outing was not by any means as strong by the end of the season. In 1955 there was a different story, for the Daimler-Benz factory really put every effort into their racing program and the Mercedes-Benz team got even stronger. In 1954 they had set the pace, and their rivals had managed to keep up and occasionally ahead, but in 1955 they swept all before them in one of the greatest seasons of technical development that Grand Prix racing had ever seen.

The first step they took was to get Stirling Moss into the team, as he had showed the ability to challenge Fangio during the previous season and there is no better place for serious opposition than

Familiar scene in 1955: Fangio 1st, Moss 2nd. Both driving Mercedes-Benz W196 Grand Prix cars

in your own team. Throughout 1955 the Grand Prix scene became one of 1st Fangio, 2nd Moss, with only a few lengths between them, these two drivers dominating races in a perfect demonstration of team driving.

It had become obvious to the Daimler-Benz designers that the 1954 car was not ideal for every racing circuit, and that it would pay to have different cars for different circuits, so two new chassis frames were built. The first had a wheelbase of 87 inches against the $92\frac{1}{2}$-inch wheelbase of the 1954 cars, and the second 1955 car was even shorter, with a wheelbase of 85-$\frac{1}{4}$ inches, built especially for such circuits as the twisty one at Monte Carlo. On the very short chassis cars there was not room for the front brakes to be mounted inboard between the radiator and the front of the engine, so the complete front of the chassis was redesigned and the brakes were mounted on the hubs in the conventional fashion. Due to this redesigning these short chassis cars were quite a lot lighter than the 1954 cars. Throughout the season the team drivers were able to have a choice of car for which ever circuit they were racing on, while the streamlined and un-streamlined body styles were also available on the medium-length chassis and the long chassis.

With all this material available, backed up by the biggest racing workshop and team of mechanics and technicians ever seen in racing, the Mercedes-Benz team eventually took complete command of Grand Prix racing, leaving all the opposition struggling along behind. Fangio was again World Champion—driving Mercedes-Benz cars in every race, and winning the Grand Prix events of Argentina, Belgium, Holland, and Italy—while Moss won the British Grand Prix. Throughout the season they only failed once to win, and that was at Monte Carlo, where all three cars retired with engine trouble of a similar nature. In the British Grand Prix they entered four cars, driven by Moss, Fangio, Kling and Taruffi, and they finished 1-2-3-4 in that order.

In other races they were invariably occupying all the leading positions until one or other of the cars broke down, for they were not 100% reliable all the season, but with as many as four cars competing and with Fangio and Moss as the main drivers, victory was as near to being certain as is possible in this uncertain business. During the season they took on other drivers, either for a specific race or as reserves, and among these were the American John Fitch and the Frenchman Andre Simon. For their sports car team of 300 SLR models, which were mechanically identical to the Grand Prix cars except for a larger engine capacity, they also took on the British drivers Collins and Titterington, the Frenchman Levegh and the young German driver Wolfgang von Trips.

Since their first appearance in the 2½-litre Formula 1 in July of 1954 to the end of 1955 the Mercedes-Benz team competed in 13 Grand Prix events, of which they won ten, were soundly beaten twice and failed to finish a single car on one occasion. Altogether they entered 42 cars in this period and of these only 15 failed to finish. With this record behind them, and having expended every effort and made use of the entire resources of the great Stuttgart factory, the directors of Daimler-Benz decided to retire from racing and turn their concentration to the production of passenger cars. So the silver Grand Prix cars were put away and the army of technicians and mechanics turned their attention to other things, leaving the Grand Prix field open to the opposition in 1956.

11. THE BRITISH SHOW THEIR HEADS

The 1956 season proved to be a strangely mixed one, starting off with Ferrari having so much useful material to draw from that his vision became fogged and he hardly knew which way to turn. Maserati was still developing its 250F car, which was basically very sound, and was paying off by concentrating on the one design. Gordini was fast running out of money and his new eight-cylinder car was dropping back due to lack of development, while in England the three main constructors were showing every possibility of challenging the Italians.

Vanwall brought out an entirely new car, though retaining the same engine and gearbox, and this new model struck a new note on aerodynamics as applied to racing cars, being without doubt the best attempt yet at combining the necessity of clear vision of the front wheels with a clean body-line, good penetration, and low frontal area. Mechanically the Vanwall was also in a strong position, for its 4-cylinder engine was fitted with fuel-injection of Bosch conception, which was functioning well, and its braking was superior to most of its rivals. Connaught had developed their B-series cars into sound raceworthy propositions, though they lacked sheer power from their engine, which was basically of Alta design. B.R.M. were showing great speed from their small and compact 4-cylinder car, but were still lacking in reliability and road-holding. In France the revered name of Bugatti was preparing to re-enter Grand Prix racing with a revolutionary design which had the engine mounted transversely in the chassis, just behind the driving seat. This engine was an eight-cylinder, twin-overhead camshaft unit of not-very-advanced design. However, this project was virtually still-born, appearing only once at a race track, and then being quite hopeless.

With Ferrari trying to decide whether to use the D50 Lancia in its original form, to modify it, or to use the engine in his own chassis, it was the opportunity for Maserati to take the lead. But it was not long before the Maranello engineers drew conclusions from their experiments and began a steady development of the original Lancia design, their main objective being to make the car easier to drive. As raced by Lancia the roadholding was of a high order, but critical when reaching its limit, and called for great finesse from the drivers.

Ferrari made many modifications, especially to the rear suspension and weight distribution, moving the fuel tanks from the panniers to the tail of the car, though he retained the pannier shape to the bodywork. Quite an amount of weight was added to the car without any great increase of power being obtained from the engine, so that though the roadholding was improved the overall gain was not outstanding. He gained successes mostly by having made the car more raceworthy and improving its reliability. Between Ferrari and Maserati the 1956 season was essentially Italian, and though the Lancia-based cars came out on top, the Maserati were not far behind. In the Modena works of Maserati it had been a season of experiment, concurrent with racing the well-proven 250F, and work was done on fuel-injection systems, aerodynamic bodywork for chosen circuits, improved braking systems, power increases by use of oxygen-bearing fuels, and a new 12-cylinder engine design. All told, the Orsi concern was kept very busy.

During the season's racing two significant features made themselves felt, the first being the obvious threat from the green cars of Great Britain. On more than one occasion the Vanwall pressed hard on the Italian cars, and given a little more luck it could have achieved a victory, and there was no doubt among the Italians that this British car was exceedingly fast. In addition, the British Grand Prix cars were increasing in numbers and whereas it used to be rare to see a green car on the starting grids of Europe, they were now beginning to mingle with the red cars and had already ousted the blue cars of France, the Bugatti being a miserable failure and Gordini being forced out for financial reasons.

There was little doubt that the British cars were almost the technical equal of the Italians, especially as regards chassis design, though they were not yet the equal on engine design. But the main problem was that they were lacking experience in Grand Prix racing. This experience cannot be bought and can only be acquired the hard practical way, but it was obvious that the English were learning very quickly indeed.

The other significant factor during the 1956 season was concerned with a new Formula that was announced by the F.I.A. This was a Formula 2 to come into operation in 1957, and to be subsidiary to the existing Formla 1. It was a very simple Formula, demanding a maximum engine size of 1500cc unsupercharged and calling for the engines to run on straight gasoline, and as it had already been announced that straight gasoline would come into force for Grand Prix cars in 1958, this new Formula 2 could be looked upon as an experimental avenue for those interested.

Although there was no intention of holding Formula 2 events until 1957, the English jumped the gun with a race for this category at Silverstone halfway through the 1956 season, and the Cooper Car Company, which had been squeezed out of Grand Prix racing by the entry of the big firms, was quick to build a car for this new category. Essentially builders of small racing cars, Cooper had litle difficulty in building a Formula 2 car and fortunately the Coventry-Climax engine company had just produced a new 1500cc racing engine which they were quick to acquire. On the medium-fast Silverstone circuit the little car was most impressive, being only a little slower than the Formula 1 cars, and interest everywhere was aroused in this new Formula. But this did not come at the expense of Formula 1, as in 1951-53, for the 2½-litre cars were well in their stride and competition and development was proceding at a reasonable pace.

A Maserati 6 cylinder 250F Grand Prix engine with two overhead camshafts, two
magnetos, three dual-throat Weber carburetors and six-branch exhaust system

12. FERRARI HAS TROUBLES;
MASERATI DROPS OUT

The Scuderia Ferrari started off the 1957 season with the Lancia
cars more or less unchanged from the previous year. They suffered
numerous troubles, however, especially with clutches, for the cars
were now producing more power and were also weighing quite a
lot more than in the days of the original design. While this was
happening Maserati forged ahead, for they had produced a much
lightened version of the 250F car, but still retained that nice degree
of balanced weight distribution which gave the car such excellent
handling properties, while the six-cylinder engine still had adequate
power and—more important—it was smooth and flexible throughout its power range.

The V8 Lancia engine, on the other hand, had a tendency to
require plenty of r.p.m. before power was developed, which made
it a fussy engine to drive. With a view to the forthcoming change
of regulations regarding fuel for Grand Prix racing, the Ferrari
engineers concentrated on running the Lancia engines on a fairly

mild alcohol mixture, whereas Maserati, living for the day, went on to the use of oxygen-bearing mixtures, thereby developing more and more power as the season went on. The races in the beginning of the season were dominated by the Italians, for the English did not join in until quite late and the sole representative from France, the Gordini, was fast fading out of the picture—the cost of racing and developing his eight-cylinder car becoming too great.

Vanwall and B.R.M. were looking forward to a season of great improvement, the former having spent most of the time building up more cars and spare units so that they could start the season with a sound backing for the team, while B.R.M. was still on development work, especially as regards the engine. The third British team, Connaught, was in difficulties as its financial backer had had to give up, and though it started the season with the B-series cars, the team soon had to give up before bankruptcy overtook it. This was another case like Gordini. Connaught was a small firm with many good ideas, but were unable to carry them through due to financial limitations, and they had gradually dropped back until they got left behind in the race for survival.

However the general scene did not change unduly, for with the going of Connaught a new name appeared in Formula 1, that of Cooper. Their little Formula 2 car with its engine mounted behind the driver had proved so successful and so fast on twisty circuits that they persuaded Coventry-Climax to build larger engines for Formula 1 events. This was done by increasing the bore and stroke of 1500cc engine as far as the castings would allow, which gave a capacity of 1.9 litres, and still being the same size outwardly the unit fitted straight into the Formula 2 car and Coopers entered it for Grand Prix events. Being 0.6 litres down on their rivals they could hardly hope to challenge them directly, but were banking on reliability and their speed round twisty corners to make up for this.

The Ferrari team was getting into a difficult situation with the Lancia-based cars, having altered them out of all recognition from the original D50 so that only the engine and gearbox/final drive assembly remained the same, and they were definitely falling behind in the horsepower race and Maserati were dominating the scene. However, this was not to continue, for as had been seen the previous year, the Vanwall was fast proving a menace to the Italian cars, and the beginning of the 1957 season showed that it was becoming more and more of a threat. By mid-season the picture had reached the situation we saw in 1951 when the downfall of the 158 Alfa Romeo by the unsupercharged 4½-litre Ferrari was inevitable. Now the downfall of both Italian teams, Maserati and Ferrari, was inevitable and at the hand of the Vanwall.

After one very near miss, victory finally came its way at the British Grand Prix, and this was followed by two more rousing victories in Italy—at Pescara and in the Italian Grand Prix at Monza. This defeat by the green Vanwalls was demoralizing the Italians, Ferrari being desperate by the end of the season and Maserati straining their 6-cylinder cars beyond all reasonable limits. Not only were Vanwalls winning but they were being backed up by B.R.M. who were hot on their heels, and all the time the little Coopers were adding fuel to fire by simply being around.

From a scene of complete domination by the German Mercedes-Benz, the 2½-litre Formula had swung through a period of Italian domination and had now reached a point where there was every possibility of the British taking over. Throughout the season Maserati had been experimenting with a new 12-cylinder engine of vee formation, having twin overhead camshafts to each bank of cylinders and running as high as 10,000 r.p.m. It relied on crankshaft speed to produce the power, of which there was plenty— over 300 b.h.p. being claimed—but it was a very difficult engine for the driver to handle, and the more flexible 6-cylinder unit was still their mainstay in racing.

The new Formula 2 had gotten under way in the beginning of the season, and though it never showed any signs of becoming of first class importance, it went from strength to strength. Naturally Cooper was well ahead at the start, having proven the car the year before, but the team was challenged by another British firm who had had a lot of sports car racing experience. This was Lotus, who used the same type of engine as Cooper—the Coventry-Climax— but in their case they fitted the engine at the front on more con-ventional lines. Convention ended at that point, for the Lotus was

1957 Cooper with rear mounted Coventry-Climax 4 cylinder engine. Driver: Roy Salvadori.

bristling with small innovations, mostly aimed at ultra-light weight and overall smallness, which the car certainly achieved.

Of the Italian constructors only Ferrari showed any serious interest in Formula 2, designing an entirely new car, though much of it was based on knowledge gained with the Lancia cars. This 1½-litre job had a truly magnificent little engine—a wide angle vee 6-cylinder layout with two overhead camshafts to each bank of three cylinders, with three double-choke carburetors mounted in the middle of the vee. The chassis was a scaled down Ferrari/Lancia, as was the transmission and suspension, and this little car—though large in comparison with the Lotus—was an extremely powerful and solid miniature Grand Prix car. It only raced twice, once in a small Italian race where it finished just behind the Lancia engined cars.

It proved 100% reliable and on a slow twisty circuit it was very nearly the equal of the 2½-litre cars; in fact, Ferrari was discovering what Cooper had found out the year before. The Formula 2 Ferrari then ran in a big event for this new category, at Rheims in France, and won after a hard fight with the Coopers. The car did not run again, but it had given Ferrari great encouragement and started a new train of thought. It was quite obvious to him that the Lancia-based Formula 1 cars were now out-dated and had reached the limit of their development, which was interesting when you remember how the original design had been laid out in 1954.

As designed and built by Lancia, the D50 was intended to have a very short life, everything being pared down to the minimum in weight and size with no room left for long-term development. Ferrari had stretched development over three years, without making any very serious gains, but seemingly going round in circles and it is more than likely that if Lancia had continued racing they would have brought out a new design after perhaps two seasons.

The Lancia/Ferrari

After struggling to make the 4-cylinder Super Squalo Ferrari keep up with the opposition in 1954 and 1955, Enzo Ferrari was more than happy to take over the entire team of Lancia D50 cars in the middle of 1955. When the season finished he set to work to make the best use of all the material available, and tried experiments with modified Lancia cars and with Lancia engines in his own cars, finally settling on a modified Lancia as the best basis for his 1956 season. The main alterations were made to weight distribution, in order to make the car easier to drive, though it was not necessarily any better than the original layout, and by the time the Lancia/Ferrari took its final form from the Scuderia Ferrari it was a lot heavier than the cars that appeared at Barcelona in 1954. The design of the engine was such that it did not allow for a great deal of development work, and, with the extra weight added, its 1956 performance was little better than in 1954, though it was much easier for the drivers to control so lap times did improve.

This was typical of Ferrari, for he had enormous practical knowledge about what could be done and what was desirable for winning races, and whereas the Lancia was designed mostly from theory with little or no regard for the short-comings of the racing driver and racing in general, Ferrari modified them to be more practical. There was a very strong team of drivers for these cars, consisting of Fangio, Collins, Musso, Castellotti and Gendebien, and Fangio won the first two races of the season, in South America. After a bout of clutch trouble, due mainly to it being mounted at the rear of the transmission in unit with the gearbox/final drive housing and in consequence being rather small in diameter, the cars began to go well again. But at Monte Carlo, where four cars were entered and proved very fast, trouble was rife. Fangio bent his car early on in the race, and in doing so caused Musso to crash, while Castellotti retired with a recurrence of the clutch trouble. He took over Fangio's bent car and the team leader took over from Collins and eventually finished 2nd.

In the Belgian Grand Prix there were five Lancia/Ferraris. They were driven by Fangio, Collins, Castellotti, Paul Frere and Andre Pilette, the last two being Belgian drivers. Although the cars did not dominate the meeting, they did at one point get into the position of being 1-2-3-4 and 6th due to their rivals having trouble, but then *they* had trouble and both Fangio and Castellotti retired with broken transmissions, leaving Collins to win, followed by Frere in 2nd place.

At the French Grand Prix another shuffle of drivers took place and Fangio, Collins and Castellotti were joined by the Marquis de Portago and Oliver Gendebien, so that it seemed as if Ferrari was out to win races by sheer weight of numbers. The first three members of the team led the race in a close bunch, serene in their command of the situation, until one of the Vanwall cars got amongst them, and then they had to drive hard to regain command of the race. Back in the lead once more Fangio had a fuel line break and the stop to have it repaired dropped him back to 4th position, once more leaving Collins to win, ahead of Castellotti.

Both the new drivers failed to finish, de Portago breaking his gearbox and Gendebien his clutch. These continual breakages rather indicated that the original Lancia design of ultra-light weight had not allowed room for development in either power or weight, both of which were being increased by Ferrari. Only four cars were entered for the British Grand Prix, the Belgian driver Gendebien being dropped, and in the Silverstone race the cars did not perform up to standard, for the average speed of the circuit seemed to be wrong for the handling characteristics of the cars. On slow and twisty circuits they were alright, and also on very fast circuits, but on a medium speed circuit like Silverstone they did not handle at all well. However, thanks to the misfortunes of other teams, Fangio was able to win and Collins finished 2nd, but it was a very lucky success and not at all deserved.

The cars were much better suited for the German Grand Prix at the Nurburgring and five were entered, with Musso returning after a spell in the hospital following a sports car crash. Fangio and Collins dominated the race to begin with, running in that nose-to-tail fashion that had been a feature of the Fangio-Moss pair in the Mercedes-Benz team of 1955. After a while Collins had to stop as his car developed a fuel leak, and this left Fangio to go on and win at his ease, the other members of the team retiring, so that of five starters on Lancia/Ferraris, only one finished. But as it was in first place, the situation was not critical.

To conclude the 1956 season Ferrari entered six cars for the Italian Grand Prix at Monza. The drivers were to be Fangio, Collins, Musso, Castellotti, de Portago and Count von Trips from Germany. This race proved to be a complete disaster for the team, for they were plagued by tire troubles and, even more serious, by breakages of steering arms. One of these broke in practice on a car von Trips was driving and he crashed heavily, reducing the car to scrap metal. During the race both Fangio and Musso had them break, while de Portago and Castellotti suffered tire blow outs which caused them to crash, and Collins had a tread come off and was delayed at the pits for a wheel change. Fangio took over from Collins and though he drove hard he could only regain 2nd place, and the Ferrari season ended on a note of complete chaos. However, during the moments when the cars were successful Fangio was able to amass sufficient points to achieve the World Championship, so the Lancia/Ferrari was successful in this respect.

The Scuderia Ferrari was now concentrating solely on the V8 Lancia engines, and building new and improved ones to the same design, but with a power output of about 280 b.h.p. However, the cars were still getting heavier. For 1957 some new chassis frames were built that were stronger and stiffer than the original Lancia, which used the engine as part of the chassis, and in consequence the 1957 cars were a lot heavier than the 1954 D50. There had been a reshuffle in the team of drivers and Fangio left to join Maserati, his place being taken by Mike Hawthorn and for the Argentine Grand Prix in January 1957 six cars were entered, driven by Collins, Hawthorn, Castellotti, Musso, a new Italian

The ultimate version of the Lancia V8 Grand Prix car as modified by the Scuderia Ferrari—the 1957 Lancia/Ferrari V8

driver named Cesare Perdisa, and Gonzalez.

But, unfortunately, the whole team suffered troubles of one sort or another, including failures of the clutch, which was still a weak point in the design, while the transmission was by no means perfect and would not withstand brutal handling. On returning to Europe the team suffered a severe setback when Castellotti was killed while doing some test driving, and as a result his friend Perdisa decided to give up racing. A redesigned Lancia/Ferrari was not built, with an entirely new front suspension and a reshaped body so that the only original Lancia parts that remained were the engine and transmission. With this new car a greater factor of reliability was achieved, so that though it was not as fast as its rivals it won on occasions by merely keeping going while others broke down.

In the Monaco Grand Prix the Scuderia suffered another setback when a series of crashes in practice and in the race demolished four of the cars, and the only result achieved was a 6th place. It seemed that without the team leadership of Juan Fangio the Ferrari team had gone to pieces. It lacked discipline and organization, and the whole set-up seemed surrounded by an air of pandemonium.

With the new rule about using aviation gas in place of alcohol fuels coming into force in 1958, Ferrari began to experiment on the V8 Lancia engines with less and less alcohol content in his fuel, and though he was down on power compared with his rivals, he achieved very good reliability. At Rouen, for the French Grand Prix of 1957, his cars finished 2nd, 3rd and 4th, driven by Musso, Collins and Hawthorn; the fourth car, driven by Trintignant retiring with magneto trouble. A race at Reims followed, and for this one Gendebien replaced Trintignant in the team. Due to a shortage of cars Musso drove an early 1956 model that was not greatly modified from the original Lancia design. Ironically, he won the race, which must have made Ferrari wonder if all his design work had been a complete waste of time.

By now the 1957 Lancia/Ferraris were finding it difficult to keep up with the opposition on both power and road holding, and the drivers seemed reluctant to go all-out because they knew that their rivals had superior machinery. In the British Grand Prix reliability was once more the keynote, and the team could do little except tag along and hope that the opposition cars would break down, which most of them did. As a result Musso was 2nd, Hawthorn 3rd and Trintignant 4th, Collins having retired with a damaged engine.

It was the same story at the Nurburgring for the German Grand Prix, though the handling was more suited to this circuit, but even so none of the team could challenge Fangio and his Maserati and Hawthorn, Collins and Musso finished 2nd, 3rd and 4th. While this reliability factor was satisfying, it would have been a bit more convincing had they displayed speed as well. Due to some internal upsets in the Maranello factory, only one car was sent to Pescara for the next big Grand Prix race, and it was driven by Musso, but though he tried as hard as he could he was forced to retire when his oil tank mounting broke.

By the end of the season the cars were just not fast enough to keep up with the Maserati and Vanwall teams, for both these had made vast improvements during the season whereas the Lancia/ Ferraris were little, if any, faster than at the beginning of the season. Four cars were entered for the Italian Grand Prix at Monza but on this fast circuit they were completely left behind. On top of that they lost some of their reliability, small failures necessitating pit-stops, so that the result was von Trips in 3rd place, two laps behind the winner, Hawthorn 6th and Musso not in the picture at all, while Collins retired with a broken engine.

This was a poor finish to the season, but already Ferrari was planning something new, and after the Monza race all the V8 Lancia based cars were junked and broken up and the Scuderia Ferrari recovered their pride with the new V6 Dino Ferrari, described elsewhere.

Ferrari reasoned that if Cooper could get away with putting a larger engine into his Formula 2 car then he could do the same, and towards the end of the 1957 season the little Ferrari was raced with an engine enlarged to just over 2 litres. Right at the end of the season one car was built with an engine of $2\frac{1}{2}$-litre capacity, still being the same V6 layout and outwardly indistinguishable from the Formula 2 car. This car was most promising and showed a surprising performance, so it was obvious where Ferrari's development would be directed for the 1958 season. In addition to having a promising design for Formula 1, which was once more a pure Ferrari, he also had a great advantage, as had Cooper, of having experience and knowledge of running his engine on non-alcohol fuels, whereas all the other Grand Prix cars would have to undergo much modification and experiment before the new season began.

Although 1957 had proved to be a Maserati winning year, and Ferrari sunk down into the back numbers, the Vanwall team was on a rising wave and the season ended with the situation very open, for B.R.M. was also showing race winning form. Grand Prix racing had now become a straight fight between Britain and Italy, while Formula 2 was hanging fire slightly, there not being many races and most people being too pre-occupied with Formula 1. However, in England enthusiasm for the new Formula was strong and as a National category there was much activity, mostly dominated by Cooper with occasional challenge from Lotus.

Grand Prix racing is a very expensive pastime, and throughout history firms have come and gone, names have been made only to end in bankruptcy, or teams have become famous only to be withdrawn just before financial ruin overtook them. To achieve success in Grand Prix racing requires enormous outlay, and even the most successful cars cannot show a profit. The whole structure of Grand Prix racing had always been that of expenditure rather than in-

114

come, and unless there is some side-issue to benefit from racing, the racing itself is nothing but one long expense. Big firms such as Alfa Romeo or Mercedes-Benz could offset the expense against production, while Ferrari and Cooper could produce sufficient competition cars for sale to just about balance things out, but for most small firms it was a case of having a source of income from somewhere other than Grand Prix racing.

Of all the firms likely to get into financial difficulties the Maserati seemed the least likely, having been in the racing game since the early 1920's and always managing to get by without having any great production to support them. However, at the end of 1957 they reached a financial crisis and were forced to announce their complete withdrawal from Grand Prix racing for 1958. Coming as it did after winning the Manufacturers Championship for 1957, and just as they were getting their 12-cylinder Grand Prix engine into a race-worthy project, it was sad indeed. Since the beginning of the Formula in 1954 many names had gone from the lists, among them Connaught, Mercedes-Benz, Lancia and Gordini, and now Maserati was to join them. However, they would not disappear completely, because the factory was prepared to help any private owners who wanted to race, and would go on with some development work. This left the Grand Prix issue between Vanwall and Ferrari, with B.R.M. ever in attendance, as was Cooper, while Lotus also followed Cooper's lead in putting an enlarged Coventry-Climax engine into their Formula 2 car.

The 250F Maserati

Having built quite a successful new car for the 1952-53 Formula 2 racing, it was only natural that the Maserati for the 1954 Formula 1 should embody many of the design features of the smaller car. After the demise of the 4CLT car the Maserati engineers withdrew from racing for a time. They started work on an entirely new car which had little in common with the 4-cylinder model, for the un-blown 2-litre car was a six-cylinder, and had double-wishbone front suspension with coal springs interspersed between the wishbones. The chassis was not a true space frame but was a compromise between a rigid ladder layout and a superstructure that also assisted rigidity. The six-cylinder engine had two overhead camshafts driven by a train of gears from the front of the crackshaft, and used three double-choke side-draught Weber carburetors, while the exhaust system was of two long tail pipes, one exhausting from cylinders 1-2-3 and the other from cylinders 4-5-6. These little engines with a bore and stroke of 76.7 mm x 72 mm were capable of very high r.p.m., often going up to 9000, and they showed a remarkable degree of reliability.

For the 1954 Formula the basic knowledge gained with the 2-litre was used to design an entirely new car known as the 250F, and Maserati made it known that while they might race themselves their main idea was to build these cars for sale to the racing public. Among the first to acquire these cars were Stirling Moss, Luigi Musso and Sergio Mantovani, while two more were brought by English drivers, and the Maserati firm in conjunction with the Argentine Automobile Club sponsored Fangio and Marimon with these new cars. In the very first race to the new Formula, Fangio was victorious using the first 250F Maserati. Having been ready before most other people with a new design, the car had success after success.

As an interim measure, some of the old 2-litre A6GCS Formula 2 cars were fitted with the new 250F engine and used in the early part of the 1954 season, Prince Bira and Harry Schell being among the owners of such cars, though both had new models towards the end of the season. Naturally enough, the factory carried on a development program running concurrently with their participation in racing, so that while the customers were limited to 7200 r.p.m. for their engines, the factory cars could run up to 8200 r.p.m. When the crankshafts and rods and valves became available to allow the customers to increase their r.p.m., the factory cars had new cylinder heads and bigger valves and could run to 8700 r.p.m. So that although there was a never-ending chase between the factory cars and the private-owners as regards power outputs, the customer was benefitting all the time, even though not always as rapidly as the factory-prepared cars.

The official drivers for the first season of this very successful and practical racing car were Fangio and Villoresi, with Musso, Mantovani, Moss and Mieres forming the rest of the team as factory-supported private owners. While the 250F had the better of the Ferrari cars for the year, it could not really beat the German Mercedes-Benz W196. But on frequent occasions it provided very strong opposition. It is still a sore point with the Maserati firm that Fangio left them at midseason to go and drive for Mercedes-Benz, for they feel that had he stayed for the whole of 1954 Maserati would have won the Manufacturers Championship. It is a reasonable supposition, for Fangio won the first two Grand Prix events for the Championship, using the new 250F, and therefore the Maserati was always in the running, using inferior drivers.

For 1955 Maserati suffered another blow when Stirling Moss left them to go and drive for the Mercedes-Benz team, but in his place they took on Jean Behra. Development work continued on the car, mostly in the search for more power, and new cars were built for the factory drivers; Behra, Musso, Mantovani and Mieres now being supported more or less completely by the Maserati firm. There were still a good many private-owners and the 1955 works cars were sold when new ones were built, and among the purchasers were Rosier, Simon, and Gould. With the Mercedes-Benz team sweeping all before it and having two really outstanding drivers, the Maserati team could only hope to tag along and try to remain in the picture.

This they did very well, never being very far behind and continually developing the car even though they could not afford the development program of the German team. During the season they experimented with fully streamlined bodywork, which was not a great success, and also perfected a five-speed gearbox and bigger brakes for the factory team cars. While 1955 was not a good year for Maserati it was not a particularly bad one, either, but in comparison with their German rivals they were terribly disorganized. For on those occasions when everything was going well the 250F showed itself to be a thoroughly sound racing car capable of still more development.

With Mercedes-Benz withdrawing from racing in 1956, the two top drivers were looking for new cars. Maserati was quick to sign-up Stirling Moss as their number one team driver, along with Behra, and Perdisa, a new young Italian. Among the experiments being worked upon for the new season was the adaptation of fuel-injection to the six cylinder engine, and also the use of nitro-methane fuels in the search for more and more power, while a new chassis was in the offing.

The team continued to be somewhat disorganized with the result that they did not win as many races as they should have, but one that was outstanding was the Monaco Grand Prix which Stirling Moss led from start to finish in a truly immaculate drive, the car performing perfectly. This, however, was followed by chaotic conditions once again with wheels breaking off at Spa and badly prepared cars at Reims.

After wasting a great deal of time and energy with the fuel-injection system, it was decided to return to Weber carburetors, for though the fuel-injected car had won a small race at Goodwood it had never out-performed the normal 250F cars. Continuing their policy of the previous years, the 1955 factory team cars were sold, and among the new owners were Piotti, Godia, Halford, two Italian private teams called the Scuderia Centro-Sud, and the Scuderia Guastalla.

At the very end of the season a Mark II 250F Maserati was built, this having the same engine but mounted at an angle to the center-line of the chassis. This allowed the driver to sit low down beside the propeller shaft instead of on top of it, and it necessitated a new rear axle/gearbox assembly, built to the same pattern as the normal 250F but with more offset in the shaft lines. This new ultra-low car was first used for the Italian Grand Prix at Monza; two were built, for Moss and Behra, and Moss drove to victory on his first outing. Rather like 1955, the 1956 season had been another one of ups and downs, the performance of the cars on the ups being first class, but on the downs chaos reigned and races were lost. The numerous private-owners were all taking advantage of the use of the factory workshops for maintaining their cars, and at times the scenes at Modena were really fantastic—with racing cars in all stages of repair in all parts of the factory only hours before a race was due to start.

This state of affairs became so critical that a stop had to be made, and in 1957 there was very definite segregation between the factory team cars and the private-owners. One or two, however, who could afford it, had the benefit of their cars being prepared in the factory team department, among these being the Spaniard Francisco Godia and Luigi Piotti. Once again there was a reshuffle of drivers and for 1957 Fangio joined the Scuderia Maserati and was supported by Behra, a rather wild Argentian named Mendi-teguy, and a new Italian driver, Giorgio Scarlatti. Abandoning the idea of the offset engine layout used in the Monza winner, three new cars were built for the 1957 team. They followed the general layout of the standard 250F but were much reduced in weight, having lighter space-frame chassis, lighter fuel and oil tanks. Compared with the original 1954 cars they were extremely lithe and sprightly, especially as the power output was approaching 280 b.h.p. and the engine speed could now run up to nearly 9000 r.p.m. in emergencies.

During the season Harry Schell joined the team and these three lightweight cars performed exceptionally well and, led by Fangio, successes came frequently to the rejuvenated Maserati 250F. After wining the Grand Prix races at Buenos Aires, Monaco, Rouen, Nurburgring, and finishing second at Pescara and Monza, Fangio annexed the World Championship for himself and the Manufac-turers Championship for Maserati. Having abandoned all development work on fuel-injection and streamlining, the firm built a new Grand Prix engine. It was a very advanced 12-cylinder in two banks of six at an included angle of 60 degrees, and a bore and stroke of 68.5 mm by 56 mm which allowed the engine to run to well over 10,000 r.p.m. and develop 310 b.h.p. This unit was re-markable in using coil ignition for its 24 spark plugs, carrying a scuttle full of ignition coils, and a battery in the cockpit.

This engine was mounted in an early 250F chassis for experi-mental purposes and, though it kept appearing for practice before races, it was a long time before it competed. Although it developed great power it was all very high r.p.m. which made it a difficult engine to handle on a twisty circuit. As the lightweight 250F models were performing exceptionally well there was little encouragement for the factory drivers to try the 12-cylinder car, but at the end of the season Behra drove it in the Italian Grand Prix at Monza and it went very well, though had to retire with overheating. For this race the engine was mounted in one of the 1956 Monza chassis' with the offset tranmission and it seemed that Maserati had at last developed something worthwhile for 1958 for the six-cylinder car, which still retained the same bore and stroke of 84 mm by 75 mm and the same 90-inch wheelbase first started in 1954.

Then, almost without warning, Maserati announced its complete withdrawal from racing. The firm had gotten into serious financial difficulties, and to go on racing would have spelt complete disaster. Consequently the 12-cylinder project was shelved and the three lightweight cars were sold to private owners, as were all the other factory team cars, though the workshops were kept open to assist the customers with race preparation. As a result of this no Maserati team took part in racing in 1958 and private-owner participation dwindled, for without the factory carrying on a development program the cars soon dropped behind in performance.

However, halfway through the season prospects brightened when Temple Buell, a wealthy American sportsman, financed the building of two new cars, still basically the 250F in design but much smaller and lighter than any previous Maserati. They retained the six-cylinder engine, the five-speed transmission, wishbone front suspension and de Dion rear suspension, but everything was reduced in size and weight to a very bare minimum. Though they did not win any races they performed well, and were driven by Fangio in his last race before he retired, and by the American drivers Masten Gregory and Carroll Shelby. Though Temple Buell financed the project, the design and work was carried out entirely by Maserati so that it did in fact represent a works Maserati, and it proved well capable of staying in the forefront even though opposed by newer designs. In 1959 it should continue to carry the name of Maserati in Grand Prix racing. Of the current Formula cars the 250F Maserati has had the longest life of any, having been created in time to win the very first race for the Formula in 1954, and after four seasons it still proved to be a strong contender, though naturally an enormous amount of development and detail change has taken place over those four years.

13. HOW THE VANWALL CAME OF AGE

The surprise of the first part of the 1958 season was undoubtedly the performance of the little Coopers with their 2.2-litre Coventry-Climax engines, for these cars were almost identical to the Formula 2 cars, though for 1958 the front suspension had been changed to double-wishbones and coil springs and new gearbox had been designed. Ferrari had his team of new cars ready, these being the Dino Type 246 model, the 2½-litre V-6 engined cars, and Maserati had sold all the 1957 team cars to private drivers and the first race proved to be a victory for the little Cooper. There followed another race on a twisty winding circuit, this time Monte Carlo, and again the Cooper was admirably suited. After Ferrari, B.R.M. and Vanwall had all taken turns at leading the race and then suffered from mechanical breakdown, it was the little Cooper that stepped in and won.

Lotus had also put a 2.2-litre Coventry-Climax engine in their Formula 2 car but it was not proving so successful as the Cooper. The Vanwall had not been greatly changed from 1957, though like all the other contestants it had been forced to have its engine modified to run on straight aviation gasoline instead of the alcohol mixtures used before. This use of straight gasoline fuel came into force at the begining of 1958, having been decreed by the F.I.A. as a new supplementary ruling for Formula 1, the engine size limitations remaining unchanged.

B.R.M. completely redesigned their chassis frame and improved the roadholding and handling of their cars enormously, while Ferrari was developing his V6 engine and getting nearly 290 b.h.p. from it. On the medium fast circuits in Europe there was little to choose between Ferrari, Vanwall and B.R.M., while on the super-fast ones the races developed into a straight fight between Ferrari and Vanwall. After winning the first two big races of the season, on very slow circuits, the Coopers were not so successful because the high speeds on the straights at such places as Rheims, Spa, Monza or Portugal saw them being left behind, while Lotus suffered from the same lack of sheer power. However, where corners played an important part these two small cars were usually in the picture, and in British National events they had a virtual monopoly, as Vanwall and B.R.M. concentrated only on the major International Grand Prix races.

In Formula 2 racing these two small factories continued to build cars for sale, and, of the two, the Cooper was decidely the most popular and most successful, practically dominating this category at smaller meetings. Ferrari raced his Formula 2 Dino 156 model on two occasions, this being a V6 and identical to the Grand Prix car in most respects, which was not surprising as the Grand Prix machine had been developed from the 1957 Formula 2 car. Porsche also showed a little interest in Formula 2, racing with a modified version of their sports car, but they ran in a limited number of events.

Towards the end of the season there were signs of renewed activity from Maserati and the 1958 version of the well-tried 250F was produced. This new car used most of the mechanical components from the 6-cylinder 250F car of the previous year, but had a new and lighter chassis frame, lighter suspension and a great saving of weight in such things as fuel tanks, radiators and oil tank. Although not an official Maserati car it represented the factory's normal development, as the Buell team was run from the Modena factory, so the close of the 1958 season saw Grand Prix racing in a healthy state, with close competition between Ferrari and Vanwall, with B.R.M. and Maserati very close behind and Cooper and Lotus ever-present and awaiting opportunities to profit from any unreliability shown by their more powerful rivals.

The Vanwall

After racing a series of Ferrari cars as a private venture, Mr. G. A. Vandervell, the British millionaire owner of the great VP automotive bearing firm, decided he would build his own car. Earlier he had supported the B.R.M. project, as he had always had the desire to see a British Grand Prix car winning races, but set up his own racing team when he realized that B.R.M. was not progressing at the rate he wanted. In 1953 he began to build a racing car utilizing much of the knowledge gleaned from the Ferraris he had bought, especially with regard to the suspension and gearbox, though the chassis frame was built for him by the Cooper Car Company.

The 4-cylinder, 2-litre engine was designed and built by the Norton Motorcycle Company, and slowly the car took shape with a view to Formula 2 racing in 1953. It never actually raced that year, but made its first appearance in a British event early in 1954, driven by Alan Brown, still as a 2-litre and called the Vanwall Special, being in the nature of a prototype. This first event was in Heats and Final form, and racing against $2\frac{1}{2}$-litre cars Brown finished 6th in his heat but had to retire in the Final when an oil pipe broke.

The car was fitted with Goodyear pattern disc brakes, as had been perfected on the $4\frac{1}{2}$-litre Ferrari "Thinwall Special," and the 4-cylinder engine used four Amal carburetors, but full fuel injection was envisaged. The car ran quite well for its first appearance and gave reasonable promise, but was not raced again until the British Grand Prix in July, as Mr. Vandervell had made it very clear that his object in building this car was to compete in the major Grand Prix races for World Championship honors. By July a new engine, to the same design, had been built of 2.3-litre capacity and this time the driver was Peter Collins, who had had experience with the big Thinwall Special.

This revised car was easily 3 seconds faster per lap on the Silverstone circuit than its predecessor, and only 5 seconds behind the leading Grand Prix contender of the time, as far as lap times were concerned. Although the car had to retire after only 17 laps with a cracked cylinder head, it showed that it was quite fast and capable of keeping up with the general run of Grand Prix cars. After this a full $2\frac{1}{2}$-litre engine was built, and it was intended that it should be used at Monza for the Italian Grand Prix, but unfortunately it gave trouble on the test-bed so the 2.3-litre engine was used. Collins finished a very respectable sixth in this full-length 300-mile Grand Prix against the most powerful opposition.

Back in England the car was entered for two short races at Goodwood, driven in one by Collins and the other by Hawthorn, and both times it gave a good account of itself. This was followed by two more short events at Aintree, driven by Hawthorn on both occasions. In the first race he finished 2nd against quite fair opposition, but in the next race retired after going off the course and choking up the radiator intake with earth and grass. The end of the 1954 season saw the Vanwall Special in Barcelona for the Spanish Grand Prix, now driven by Collins once more, but he was unfortunate to crash in practice and the rear of the car was so badly damaged that it could not start.

For 1955 the Vandervell factory built two new cars and they were given the name of Vanwall, the "Special" part of the name now being dropped. They were basically the same as the prototype car, but many detail improvements were made. The body shape was much smoother, while the 4-cylinder engine underwent a major and important change in being fitted with Bosch high-pressure fuel injection, the charge being inserted into the inlet port just behind the valve. It was not until May that the cars were ready and they ran at Silverstone, driven by Hawthorn and Ken Wharton, but neither car lived up to promise shown the previous season, Hawthorn retiring with an oil leak in the gearbox and Wharton having a rather serious crash which not only injured him but caused the car to catch fire and be burnt out.

Vandervell's aim was to field a team of three cars in all the big Grand Prix races, but the Silverstone crash rather set his plans back, and only one car was taken to Monte Carlo, driven by Hawthorn. It ran well but was not the equal of the German and Italian opposition, and after only 23 laps it had to retire with a broken control in the throttle and fuel-injection system. Following this Hawthorn again drove the car in the Belgian Grand Prix, but another retirement was forced on him when an oil leak developed in the gear box. After this he left the team, his place being taken by Harry Schell. Wharton was now fully recovered, so that for the British Grand Prix at Aintree two cars were entered.

It was here that the first signs of the true potential of the car were clearly demonstrated, for in practice Schell proved capable of lapping at speeds equal to most of the Italian cars, though not as fast as the Germans. In the race he was delayed by stalling his engine at the start and got off last, but soon overhauled a great number of the opposition and worked his way up to 8th place. At that point the accelerator pedal broke clean off and he was forced to retire, but he had shown how the Vanwall could be made to move when really pressed. Later in the race Wharton stopped with a broken oil pipe, and after it had been mended Schell took over and once more drove the Vanwall as hard as possible, and though it finished last it had been lapping at a very creditable speed, at least the equal of the Maserati cars and faster than the Ferraris and Gordinis, but nowhere near the speed of the Mercedes-Benz team.

As some of the Grand Prix events were cancelled Vanderwall ran the cars in some small British races, and Schell achieved a 2nd place at the Crystal Palace and a win at Snetterton, at which circuit Wharton finished 2nd. In September the same two drivers competed in the Italian Grand Prix but they were outclassed on speed and road holding on the Monza track, while the cars suffered mechanical breakages. However, the Vanwall team was now becoming a very serious force, for they had three complete cars with them and the supply of parts were mounting up, no expense being spared in the preparation and building of the cars. To conclude their 1955 activities the three cars were entered for the Gold Cup at Oulton Park, with Schell, Wharton and Desmond Titterington as the drivers, but only two started as Wharton was not feeling well. Schell retired with a damaged drive shaft, but Titterington ran steadily to finish in 3rd place. A little later at Castle Coombe aerodrome circuit Schell drove in two short races and won them both.

Now that the nucleus of the Vanwall Racing Team was well in stride and the engines were producing sufficient power, attention was turned to the chassis and suspension. Using a new young British designer, Colin Chapman, a completely new chassis frame of very light tubing was built, both front and rear suspension was modified, and a new five-speed gear-box built, while the engine was developed still further. A very streamlined body was designed by Frank Costin and the 1956 Vanwall was now obviously a very serious contender for top Grand Prix honors.

The first outing for the redesigned Vanwall was a race at Silverstone and for this event Stirling Moss joined the team, having no other contract for this particular race. He went out and won at record speed, giving a most convincing demonstration of the car's capabilities. Schell was in the second car and going well until a fuel-injection pipe broke and forced him out. After this initial outing Moss had to join the Maserati team, so the French driver Maurice Trintignant joined Schell on the Vanwall team and they competed at Monte Carlo. Both cars showed every promise of going well, but were eliminated from the race by minor accidents due to getting involved with other cars on this narrow twisty circuit, and Schell was battling for 2nd place at the time of his retirement. At the Belgian Grand Prix on the very fast Spa circuit, which followed the Monte Carlo race, the same two drivers took part. Although Trintignant had to retire with fuel mixture troubles, Schell finished 4th, but it had become obvious that the high-speed handling of the Vanwalls still left a lot to be desired. On sheer speed they were a match for the Maserati and Ferrari opposition, but lost ground on the 160 m.p.h. corners.

In the French Grand Prix at Reims the cars once more demonstrated their speed capabilities, but were beset by unforunate incidents. For this event a third one of the new cars was completed. Colin Chapman, the designer, was entered as driver, but he was eliminated by a crash in practice, leaving only Schell and Hawthorn as Trintignant was driving for Bugatti. Schell broke his gearbox in the opening laps and then damaged his engine, so he withdrew and took over Hawthorn's car. In a stirring drive he caught and passed the entire Ferrari team who were dominating the race. However, he could not fight off the attack of the three Italian cars and had to drop back and then a control rod to the injection pump broke and he had to stop at the pits for a repair and he eventually finished at the back of the field. But he had shown that the Vanwall was now more than the equal of the Italian cars, so that Mr. Vandervell could see his goal in sight, as the Germans had withdrawn from racing. The British Grand Prix followed at Silverstone and for this race three cars were entered—to be driven by Schell, Trintignant and Gonzalez—but it was a complete fiasco and all three retired without putting up any sort of show at all.

The next event was given a miss, in order to put right a number of faults, and a fourth car was completed, so that for the Italian Grand Prix of 1956, at Monza, three entries were made and a spare car was available in case of trouble in practice; the drivers were Schell, Trintignant and Taruffi. In the race Schell battled furiously against the leading opposition, many times actually leading the race, and the Vanwall was undoubtedly faster on maximum speed than its rivals but it still lacked high-speed road holding. This great fight came to an end when an oil leak caused the gearbox/final drive unit to seize, but it was now very clear that a victory was within sight for the Vanwall team if reliability could be achieved in the small details of the car. The other two cars both retired, one with a similar fault to that on Schell's car and the other with a broken front suspension. This ended the 1956 season for the Vanwall team, but it faced 1957 sure in the knowledge that it was very close to achieving Mr. Vandervell's ambition of a Grand Prix victory for a British car.

A major step forward was taken in 1957 when Stirling Moss joined the team, and he had as number two driver an up-and-coming young Englishman in Tony Brooks. The cars were unchanged from the previous year, apart from a few details, and most effort was put into building up a strong reserve of spare engines, gearboxes, suspension and so on in order that the drivers should be backed up by cars in first class condition. Rather than sign on an inferior driver to team up with Moss and Brooks, the Vanwall team rested with two drivers until such time as a third member could be found who was of equal caliber.

The 1957 Vanwall Grand Prix car, showing the smoothness of line of this British racing car

Unlike previous seasons, the team was ready from the word go and took part in all the major events of the year, plus one or two lesser events as experimental try-outs. The cars proved immensely fast but were still not reliable, losing victories due to small items failing, but at Monte Carlo Brooks finished a worthy 2nd after Moss had crashed. At the French Grand Prix at Rouen the team was in a sad plight for both Moss and Brooks were unwell, leaving it with two entries and no drivers. At the last minute Roy Salvadori and Stuart Lewis-Evans filled the gap, but neither made very much impression in their first race with the cars.

These two drove again the following weekend at Reims, and while Salvadori was not getting used to the car, Lewis-Evans was making great progress and actually led the race completely unchallenged until an oil leak obscured his visibility and he had to slow down, finishing 3rd. It was now just a matter of time before victory came to the Vanwall, for even with new drivers it was a match for any of the opposition.

Vandervell's greatest day came at Aintree on the occasion of the British Grand Prix. Moss was fit once more, Brooks was capable of driving, and a third car was entered for Lewis-Evans so now there was a full Vanwall team able to give battle to all-comers. From the

The Italian Grand Prix of 1957 showing the Vanwall team dominating the starting grid

fall of the flag Moss shot away into the lead and left everyone behind and at last it looked as though a Vanwall was going to achieve a runaway victory.

However, after less than one quarter of the race had been run the ignition system on the leader's car gave trouble and he had to stop at the pits. It could not be cured so he took over from Brooks, restarting the race in 9th place and then gave a superb demonstration of high-speed driving and romped through the field, forcing the opposition to go faster than they wanted to until they broke down, whereupon Moss took the lead and held it to the finish. Brooks struggled on in the sick car but finally had to give up, while Lewis-Evans was robbed of a certain 2nd place by a mechanical fault which delayed him at the pits so that he could finish no higher than 7th. At last Tony Vandervell's dream had come true, and where more fitting than on British soil in the Grand Prix of his own country.

This joy was short-lived for the next race was on the tortuous Nurburgring and the same three drivers took part but were severely hampered by road holding that was not adequate for the bumpy circuit. The best they could do was for Moss to finish 5th and Brooks 9th, while Lewis-Evans crashed when his gearbox lost all its oil.

After one victory and one set-back, the team went to Pescara in Italy and here Moss trounced all the opposition and won the race with ease, at record speed being over 3 minutes ahead of the second man, who was Fangio with a Maserati. Brooks was forced out when a piston broke and Lewis-Evans was delayed by tire trouble and could only manage 5th place, but these were trifles in comparison with the wonderful victory achieved by Stirling Moss.

There was no doubt that the Vanwall team now had the Italian cars at their mercy, and in the Italian Grand Prix the three cars occupied the first three places on the starting grid, decided on practice times. Once again it was Moss who set the pace and ably backed up by his team-mates he fought hard against Fangio and Behra on Maseratis, finally vanqushing them and winning the race, but it was at the expense of the other Vanwalls. Brooks had to stop because of a gearbox oil leak and could only finish 7th, though he did record a new lap record, while Lewis-Evans had to retire with a damaged engine. In the final race of 1957 at Casablanca, in Morocco, the three cars ran again, but were reduced to two at the start as Stirling Moss was taken ill. Without their team leader the other two were never able to challenge the opposition and Brooks eventually retired with magneto trouble, but Lewis-Evans was able to finish in 2nd place though at no time did he challenge the leader.

For 1958 most of the preparation time was spent in converting the engines to run on aviation gas instead of the alcohol mixture with a touch of nitro-methane used previously, for the F.I.A. rules for 1958 banned alcohol for Formula 1. The cars were unchanged in general conception, though some detail lightening was carried out, and the same three drivers were retained. Their first race was at Monte Carlo and proved to be a complete fiasco, all three cars retiring, though they had the consolation of having led the race for quite a time, but lack of reliability in a design now in its third year seemed unreasonable.

This was more than recompensed at the Dutch Grand Prix which followed, for Stirling Moss led from start to finish in a perfect demonstration of Vanwall superiority, but this clear-cut victory was gained at the expense of the retirement of the other two cars. The Belgian Grand Prix was their next race and after Moss had led and then broken the engine, it was Brooks who stepped in and dominated the race to gain another decisive victory. Lewis-Evans was luckier this time and finished in 3rd place.

They went from Belgium to France for the French Grand Prix and on the very fast Reims circuit victory seemed assured but Ferrari found a lot more speed and the best Vanwall performance was by Moss who finished 2nd. After this beating the team suffered one at Silverstone on the occasion of the British Grand Prix, for Moss broke his engine in his efforts to catch the leading Ferrari, Lewis-Evans could only manage 3rd and Brooks was a long way behind.

At Nurburgring, for the German Grand Prix, their task seemed hopeless in view of the troubles experienced in 1957, but they showed that they had learned by experience. Moss led for a time and then went out with magneto trouble, and Brooks once more drove a superb race to gain Vanwall its third victory of the season. In the Portuguese Grand Prix Moss was truly on form and gave another demonstration run, winning all the way, while Lewis-Evans backed him up with a fine 2nd place. Although Ferrari supplied plenty of opposition at Monza on the occasion of the Italian Grand Prix, the Vanwall team was more than a match for them, and Moss set the pace, only to retire with gearbox trouble, while Lewis-Evans suffered from engine overheating, but Brooks fought the Italians to chalk up the fifth Grand Prix victory of 1958.

The season ended at Casablanca and though both Brooks and Lewis-Evans had engine trouble, the latter dying as a result of injuries received in a crash, Stirling Moss showed his true driving style by winning the race with ease against very strong opposition. This was the sixth great victory for the team in one year, and they proudly took the title of Champion Manufacturer of Grand Prix racing for 1958.

The Ferrari Dino 246

Enzo Ferrari hit upon the idea of the Dino 246 model more by accident than design, for the original conception was for a Formula 2 car of 1500cc. Having built the prototype, he suddenly realized that it could be enlarged in a capacity to 2½-litre without increasing the general size of the car. The Formula 2 project with its V6 cylinder engine was in effect a scaled down version of the 1957 Lancia/Ferrari as far as the chassis layout and suspension were concerned, and much of the inspiration for the beautiful little 1500cc engine came from Enzo Ferrari's son Dino Ferrari.

Unfortunately an illness caused his death before the completion of the car, and in memory of his son Ferrari named the V-6 engine the Dino. For its capacity it produced a great many horsepower, far in excess of other Formula 2 cars, but it weighed a great deal more than its British rivals. With the Lancia/Ferrari V8 cars at the end of their development towards the close of the 1957 season, work was begun on enlarging the Dino engine, at first by the simple expedient of increasing the bore until just over 2 litres was achieved, and later by increasing both bore and stroke until 2½ litres was reached, and it was all done without increasing the overall dimensions of the power unit.

At the end of 1957 two enlarged cars raced at Modena in a small Grand Prix, driven by Musso and Collins, and they finished 2nd and 4th in that order, against quite strong Maserati and B.R.M. opposition, which proved that Ferrari was onto a good idea with his enlarged Formula 2 car. The two cars ran again at Casablanca, and though they could not challange the faster cars on this high-speed circuit in practice, they had an advantage in the race due to weighing a lot less than their rivals when fully laden for a full length Grand Prix.

Collins led for quite a time and then lay 2nd, but was finally put out of the race when he overshot a corner and bent the car, while Hawthorn was in trouble with a broken gearbox. However, bearing in mind that these engines were running on straight gasoline against their rivals who were on nitro-alcohol mixtures for the last time, Ferrari was more than satisfied and started the 1958 season with a huge advantage over most of his rivals. Throughout the 1958 season the Dino Ferraris were consistent performers, always in the running though not always winning, but Hawthorn made a remarkable number of fastest practice laps and record race laps, and by a consistent performance throughout the season he won the World Championship using the Dino 246 Ferrari.

He only had one victory, in the French Grand Prix, while Collins won the British Grand Prix, but the cars were invariably well-placed and should have won more races. One of the weak points of the car was the clutch, for like the Lancia/Ferrari it was enclosed at the back of the car in conjunction with the gearbox, and was not as large as it might have been. Due to this, it would not stand a lot of abuse and in the German and Italian Grand Prix races Hawthorn had trouble with it, though he managed to nurse his car into 2nd place at Monza. The American driver Phil Hill joined the team at the end of the season and took to the Dino Ferrari like the proverbial duck, putting up two great drives, at Monza and Casablanca, finishing 3rd on both occasions with a lap record for the Italian track thrown in for good measure.

The Dino Ferrari in its first season as a full Grand Prix car enabled Hawthorn to win the World Championship, but it failed to get the Manufacturers Championship for Ferrari and it also caused some grief in the team. In the French Grand Prix Luigi Musso crashed and was killed and in the German Grand Prix Peter Collins did the same, and both these deaths were at the wheel of a Dino. Since the original Formula 2 experiment the cars had new chassis frames that were slightly heavier, but much stronger, and such things as drive shafts, clutches and brakes all had to be strengthened to take the added power of the $2\frac{1}{2}$-litre engine. By the end of the 1958 season and after only 12 months of development, the Dino engine was developing nearly 290 b.h.p. at 8500 r.p.m. and in emergencies it could run as high as 9600 r.p.m. without breaking. It is true to say the strength of a racing car lies in its engine, and in the V-6 Dino engine Ferrari had a truly strong car.

Already the 1954 Formula for Grand Prix cars had been extended beyond its normal three-year span, it having been mutually agreed by members of F.I.A. that it should continue until the end of 1960. At the close of 1958 the new rules for the 1961-64 Formula for Grand Prix cars were announced, thus giving manufacturers two whole years during which to design and build new cars. Although decided upon and voted for in the usual manner among delegates to the F.I.A., the new rules proved very unpopular with the manufacturers. This was because they demanded an engine limitation of a maximum of 1500cc and a minimum of 1300cc, with a complete ban on superchargers.

The 1954-60 Formula had seen the virtual death of supercharged engines, for though the rules permitted supercharged engines of 750cc no manufacturer took advantage of this, and all designers worked on the unsupercharged 2500cc limit. The result was that the study of supercharged engines for racing came to a complete stop in the Grand Prix world, so there was little point in continuing with a supercharged category in any new Formula. In addition to the 1300cc-1500cc capacity limits, a minimum weight of 1120 pounds was imposed, it being felt that cars such as the little Cooper and Lotus were being built on a rather flimsy and low safety factor, especially from the point of view of driver safety in the result of an accident.

Though not very popular with the British manufacturers, this new Formula would inspire competition from new firms, and already Porsche and Borgward have shown signs of taking part in Grand Prix racing in 1961, while Ferrari and Maserati will undoubtedly construct new 1½-litre cars to the new rules, having supported every Formula since they began racing. With each successive change in Formula or change in design trend in Grand Prix racing someone has fallen by the wayside, and invariably someone new has risen to take their place. At present we no longer have Alfa Romeo, Mercedes-Benz, H.W.M., Talbot, Connaught or Gordini competing, but we have in their place Vanwall, B.R.M., Cooper and Lotus, while Ferrari and Maserati have been consistently in the Grand Prix picture. With Porsche and Borgward becoming interested in the new Formula, and possibly Osca— while Mercedes-Benz and Gordini may return to the scene—we can be assured of continued technical development through the field of Grand Prix racing.

Tests show:

Unleaded gasoline cuts engine wear

Protect your car's engine with clear white unleaded **AMOCO-GAS!**

In a recent independent test,* car engines run 20,000 miles on non-leaded gasoline showed substantially less wear than similar engines run under similar conditions with leaded fuel.

Calipered cylinder bore wear was 31.6% *less* with unleaded gasoline. Piston ring wear was cut—ring gap increase was 52.2% *less;* side clearance increase was 74% *less.* Bearing wear (weight loss) was 15.4% *less.*

The reduced wear is attributed to the absence of abrasive lead compounds on cylinder walls, rings and bearings. In addition to causing wear these lead compounds often foul spark plugs and valves and upset spark timing.

This backs up the preference of sports car racers, foreign and economy car drivers and dealers for white, unleaded Amoco-Gas—America's only unleaded, premium octane motor fuel.

Amoco-Gas, *refined* to high octane without the use of lead additives, assures complete freedom from lead fouling, the abrasive action of lead deposits, and the corrosive effect of lead compounds on mufflers. Engines run cleaner, smoother, with fewer expensive repairs and costly overhauls. *Details on request.*

Experts who know use Amoco

AMERICAN OIL COMPANY